# THOSE TERRIBLE MIDDLE AGES

RÉGINE PERNOUD

# Those Terrible
# Middle Ages

## *Debunking the Myths*

Translated by
Anne Englund Nash

IGNATIUS PRESS     SAN FRANCISCO

Title of the French original:
*Pour en finir avec le Moyen Age*
© 1977 Éditions du Seuil

Cover photograph by Ruggero Vanni
Notre Dame Cathedral in Laon: Nave
© Vanni Archive/CORBIS

Cover by Roxanne Mei Lum

# CONTENTS

# FOREWORD

More than a quarter century ago exasperation led one of history's most distinguished scholars to sit down and write an extended essay on her pet peeve. The result was this book, which contains rich veins of information for the amateur as well for the professional scholar. It is a book written in a brisk and at times petulant style.

The Middle Ages—those one thousand years of Western history between 500 and 1500 A.D.—witnessed the abolition of slavery, the liberation of women, checks and balances on absolutism, artistic achievements of medieval cathedrals, inventions of the book, the musical scale, and the mechanical clock. Why is it then that the very term *Middle Ages* is equated, even in the minds of so-called educated people, with such ideas as feudal servitude, cultural darkness, massacres, famines, and plagues?

Pernoud attributes such ignorance in part to classicism, which became predominant in the sixteenth century, reached its apogee in the eighteenth, and is witnessing its demise in our own days. The revival of Roman law brought about legal standardization in the interest of centralized nation states. The Roman notion of the *jus utendi et abutendi*, the unrestricted rights of property, put an end to the legal rights enjoyed by medieval serfs and feudal lords. The result was the reintroduction of slavery, the subjection of women, the exploitation of the worker, and the rise of the absolutist state. A corollary to these political and social changes was a preoccupation with "sources" and "influences". Had not perfection been reached in the Parthenon and Venus de Milo?

The result was paralysis in literary and art criticism that has continued down to modern times.

Pernoud shows that "the Middle Ages" was not a homogenous block and she suggested that it should be divided into sections that scholars twenty-five years later have, with some modifications, accepted: (500–950) Merovingian Frankish; (950–1300) Feudal age; (1300–1500), the true Middle Ages. She argues well that the Middle Ages were in some ways closer to our own age than were those ages formed by the classical spirit.

Even though progress has been made in Medieval studies since the publication of this book, which was written primarily for a French public, nevertheless, it is a worthwhile study for the ordinary education reader and a must for students.

Cornelius Michael Buckley, S. J.
University of San Francisco

I

# "MIDDLE AGES"

I had recently been put in charge of the museum of French history in the National Archives when a letter was sent to me requesting: "Could you tell me the exact date of the treaty that officially put an end to the Middle Ages?" Along with the subsidiary question: "In what city were the plenipotentiaries gathered who prepared this treaty?"

Not having saved this letter, I can only give the substance of it, but I can guarantee that this is accurate; its author was seeking a quick reply, for, he said, he needed these two pieces of information for a conference he was expecting to give at a date that was quite close at hand.

I have sometimes found myself writing this conference in my head for my own amusement. And without difficulty: one need only place end to end what one reads, sees, and hears every day about the "Middle Ages".[1] Now the medievalist, if he has his mind set on collecting foolish quotations on the subject, finds himself overloaded by everyday life. Not a day goes by that one does not hear some reflection of this kind: "We aren't in the Middle Ages any more", or "That's a return to the Middle Ages", or "That's a medieval mentality."

[1] "Middle Ages" should always be in quotation marks; I am adopting the expression here in order to conform to current usage.

And these come in all kinds of circumstances: to recall the claims of the MLF or to deplore the consequences of a strike by the EDF[2] or when one is led to voice general ideas about demography, illiteracy, education, and so forth.

It all begins early: I remember having had occasion to accompany a nephew to one of his classes where the parents are admitted so that afterward they can work with their children. He must have been seven or eight years old. When the time came for the recitation of history, here, word for word, is what I heard:

> *Teacher:* What are the peasants of the Middle Ages called?
> *Class:* They are called serfs.
> *Teacher:* And what did they do, what did they have?
> *Class:* They were sick.
> *Teacher:* What illnesses did they have, Jérôme?
> *Jérôme* (very serious): The plague.
> *Teacher:* And what else, Emmanuel?
> *Emmanuel* (enthusiastically): Cholera.

"You know your history very well", the teacher concluded placidly. "Let's go on to geography."

Since that happened several years ago and the nephew in question has by now attained the age of majority according to the civil code, I believed that surely things had changed since then. But here I was, several months ago (July 1975), going for a walk with the granddaughter of one of my friends (Amélie, seven years old), when the latter threw out at me joyfully:

"You know, at school, I'm learning about the Middle Ages."

---

[2] Mission Laïque Française (an organization founded in 1902, devoted to the teaching and dissemination of French language and culture) and Electricité de France (France's national electrical power utility).—TRANS.

"Ah, well good! And what were these Middle Ages like? Tell me."

"Well, there were (it took her a little searching before she came up with the difficult word . . .) feudal lords. And then they were making war all the time, and they went into the peasants' fields with their horses, and they spoiled everything."

An ice-cream cone then captured her attention and put an end to her enthusiastic description. That made me understand that in 1975 history was being taught exactly as it had been taught to me a half-century earlier. So much for progress.

And at the same time, it made me regret laughing out loud—which was admittedly rather uncharitable—several days earlier when I received a telephone call from a TV research assistant—now who should be more specialized in historical programs!

"I understand", she said, "that you have some transparencies. Do you have any that *represent the Middle Ages?*"

"Represent?"

"Yes, that give an idea of the Middle Ages in general: slaughter, massacres, scenes of violence, famines, epidemics . . ."

I could not keep from laughing out loud, and that was unfair. Obviously this research assistant had not gone beyond Amélie's level on the particular historical point of the Middle Ages. But how would she have gone beyond? Where would she have learned more?

\* \* \*

Up to a very recent period, it was still only by mistake, or, let us say, by chance, that one came into contact with the Middle Ages. A personal curiosity was necessary and, in order to arouse that curiosity, some impact, some encounter.

This may have been a Romanesque door, a Gothic arrow, in the course of a journey; a chance painting or a tapestry in museums or expositions; one suspected then the existence of a universe hitherto unknown. But the impact past, how was one to know more? Encyclopedias or dictionaries that one consulted contained only what was insignificant or disdainful about the period; works devoted to the period were still rare, and their data generally contradictory. We are speaking here of popular works accessible to the average public, for it is evident that scholarly works have been plentiful for a long time. But to obtain them, there was a whole series of obstacles to clear: first, access to the libraries that contained them, then, the barrier formed by the specialized language in which most of them were written. This was so much the case that the general level of knowledge can be supplied by the question that served as the basis for a meeting of the Cercle catholique des intellectuels français (Catholic circle of French intellectuals) in 1964: "Were the Middle Ages Civilized?"—without the least bit of humor: that we can be sure of at once, since it involved intellectuals who were for the most part from universities and for the most part employed. The discussions took place in Paris, on rue Madame. One hopes, for the moral comfort of the participants, that none of them, in order to return to his residence, had to pass by Notre-Dame de Paris. He might have felt a certain uneasiness. But no, let us reassure ourselves: an employed academic is, in any case, physically incapable of seeing what is not in conformity with the notions his brain exudes. Thus he would not in any way have seen Notre-Dame, even if his path took him to the Place du Parvis.

Everything is different today. The Place du Parvis itself is mobbed, every Sunday and, during the summer, every weekday as well by a crowd of young people, and some who are not so young, who listen to singers and musicians and at times dance while they listen; or who, seated on the ground, simply contemplate the cathedral. Most are not content simply to admire the exterior: Notre-Dame de Paris has found again the crowds of the Middle Ages, every Sunday, when its doors open wide at concert time. Admiring, contemplative crowds to whom the intellectual of 1964 would seem like an animal in a zoo (the old kind of zoo, of course). The reasons for this change? They are multiple. The first and most immediate is that today everyone is on the go. People move around a lot and everywhere. The medievalist cannot keep from adding: "just as in the Middle Ages", for, taking modern means of transportation into account, tourism takes the place today that pilgrimages had in former times. We start traveling precisely as people did in medieval times.

Now it happens that in France, especially, in spite of vandalism that is more serious and more methodical than anywhere else, the traces of the medieval period remain more numerous than those of all other periods put together. It is impossible to move around our homes without seeing a steeple rise up in the sky, which is enough to evoke the twelfth or thirteenth century. It is impossible to climb to a mountaintop without finding a little chapel, and one often wonders by what miracle it could spring up in such a wild, distant corner. A region like Auvergne does not contain a single important museum, but, on the other hand, what riches between Orcival and Saint-Nectaire, Le Puy and Notre-Dame-du-Port at Clermont-Ferrand! These regions, which, in the seventeenth century, stewards or governors considered a regrettable banishment, were thus in other times inhabited by a population large enough to achieve such marvels and well enough informed to conceive of them. Whether this was the function of monasteries or of popular culture matters little. Where, then, were monks recruited, if not from the people in general and from all social strata, to speak the language of the twentieth century? And besides, if Aubazine was a Cistercian convent, do we not see simple rural parishes like Brinay or Vicq (today Nohant-Vicq) endowed with Romanesque frescoes whose audacity still seems disconcerting to us today?

There is a regular flood of tourists nowadays into the edifices of the Middle Ages. Mont-Saint-Michel receives more visitors than the Louvre. Les Baux-de-Provence see lines of automobiles stretch from the place where they climb in clusters to storm the old fortress. Fontevrault, only just become accessible again to visitors, is no longer large enough to receive everyone; the abbey of Sénanque, although the monks' chant was for years heard there only through a (remarkable) audio-visual show, enjoys an uninterrupted flow. In short, we could enumerate all the regions of France, from the medieval feasts of Beauvais at the farthest borders of Picardy to those of Saint-Savin within the farthest borders of the Pyrenees: everywhere it is the same enthusiasm for an undoubtedly recent but general rediscovery.

From the sole fact that he travels, the Frenchman, who moreover has been outmatched in this regard by the Englishman, the German, the Belgian, the Dutchman—to say nothing, of course, of the American—becomes aware of his environment. And aware of what in that environment is not limited to nature. Or, rather, nature, however little he may open his eyes, appears to him already considerably transformed and brought to fruition by the use man has made of it in other times: stones, bricks, woodwork that, once assembled and put into use, played in the landscape the role of an image in a book. At the same time, he becomes aware, therefore, of the value of all that is a part of this environment. It is well past the time when the Languedocian proprietors sold off the capitals of the columns of Saint-Michel-de-

Cuxa, which today [1977] they are preparing to return from America. Well past the time when a building contractor could, without raising any protest, cut up the cloister of Saint-Guilhem-le-Désert to sell the sculpted stones separately. If it is necessary today to go to New York to find these cloisters—treated, moreover, with admirable respect—with which a museum could be made (Serrabone, Bonnefont-en-Comminges, Trie-en-Bigorre, and the two already cited of Saint-Guilhem-le-Désert and Saint-Michel-de-Cuxa as well as the chapter house of Pontaut dans les Landes), in the end one must understand that the one responsible for such displacements was not the buyer but the seller. Even at that, the sale constituted only a half-evil: one can always go to Philadelphia to see the cloister of Saint-Genis-lès-Fontaines or to Toledo to admire that of Saint-Pons-de-Thomières, but what is there to say about all that disappeared irreparably under the Empire, for example at Cluny, where what had been the largest Romanesque church of Christianity was blown up, or at Toulouse, which was, as we know, nicknamed the "capital of vandalism" and where only a few bits of the cloisters of Saint-Étienne, Saint-Sernin, and La Daurade could be saved?

A past well over with, nevertheless, and one that arouses indignation. Just as that strange habit of having those monasteries that were not destroyed transformed into prisons or barracks arouses astonishment. And that in itself indicates the extent of the movement, the relative rapidity with which it was accomplished. For, in the end, it was scarcely one hundred years ago that Victor Hugo, visiting Mont-Saint-Michel transformed into a prison, cried out: "It is like seeing a toad in a reliquary!" And even I could still see in my childhood, at the time when there was an effort to make them disappear, the little regular windows cut into the wall that had transformed the great hall of the palace of the popes in Avignon into barracks. Today, when even Fontevrault has finally been returned to itself, who then would admit that Mont-Saint-Michel or the palace of the popes could become barracks or a prison? There is still, it is true, a certain fire station on the rue de Poissy in Paris, but everyone knows that Paris will always lag behind the "provinces"!

If it manifested itself belatedly in France, the movement that pushes to rediscover, restore, and reanimate the monuments of the past will exist from now on. It has penetrated deeply; it has come to overwhelm and disturb even the authorities who had the care of those monuments up to now. Everywhere archeological clubs have opened, restoration workgroups and excavation campaigns have begun. We see admirable Romanesque edifices, even those hidden in the barely accessible countryside, recover their form and their life thanks to public and private associations of care and protection sustained, controlled, and sometimes even initiated by the local administration. I am thinking of Saint-Donat but also of the rotunda of Simiane in Haute-Provence, or even, not far from there, of the chapel of the Magdalen. Already, in that same region, the property owner who persists in piling his hay in a Romanesque or Gothic chapel—as was done for a century and a half—comes across as ignorant, behind the times. And one could cite such restoration of monuments everywhere: the palace of Rohan at Pontivy, the church of Lieu Restauré in Picardy, Château-Rocher in Auvergne, the chapel of the Templars of Fourches in the Paris region, the Blanquefort palace in Gironde—taken in hand and restored often by groups of young people acting spontaneously. It has at last been understood that in this domain, everything has to come from private initiative, followed, controlled, and encouraged by public powers—since for restoration as for excavations, properly speaking, good will cannot be enough; education, training, and supervision are necessary; in any case one can do nothing serious without them. But who would have imagined this fifty years ago? Who would have foreseen it even ten years ago (1965), when the journal *Archeologia*, in its first number, opened a column: "Where will you make an excavation this summer?" This column, at present, must be spread out each year over several issues, one no longer being enough.

Television has played a role in the development of this curiosity. In drawing attention to neglected monuments, by encouraging certain achievements, it has stimulated the interest that the general public was beginning to show for the witnesses of the past. We are thinking of certain broadcasts like the *Chefs-d'oeuvre en péril* (Masterpieces in peril) or *La France défigurée* (France disfigured), which have contributed powerfully in making a broader public sensitive to these treasures that one encounters without always being able to recognize them. By placing them within reach of all spectators, it has, at the same time, made work done previously bear fruit: that of history collections, of high-level popular works or journals. We will not cite them all. It will be enough to take as an example the Zodiac series, which undertook some twenty-five years ago to make Romanesque art better known and whose success is self-evident today. There are also numerous societies that have worked in the same direction as the Centre international d'études romanes. Or again, more recently, the Communautés d'accueil dans les sites artistiques (CASA), composed of young people, students for the most part, who are undertaking to communicate what in general only art historians know and are allowing everyone to appreciate the examination of twelfth and thirteenth-century monuments.

It is enough to say that the average Frenchman, today, no longer agrees if someone describes the sculptures of a Romanesque portal as "clumsy and awkward" or the colors of the Chartres stained-glass windows as "garish". His artistic sense is sharp enough for him to consider judgments that would not even have been discussed thirty years ago to be definitively out of date. Yet a certain gap, perhaps derived particularly from habits of mind or vocabulary, still exists between the Middle Ages that he admires any time he has occasion to and what this term Middle Ages covers for him.[3] A gap that marks the break between what he can observe directly and what escapes him through the force of circumstances because he needs an education that no one has yet given him and that only an intelligent study of history during his school years would provide him.

The Middle Ages still signifies: a period of ignorance, mindlessness, or generalized underdevelopment, even if this was the only period of underdevelopment during which cathedrals were built! That is because the scholarly research done for the past fifty years and more has not yet, as a whole, reached the public at large.

One example is striking. Not so long ago a television broadcast reported as historical the famous words: "Kill them all, God will recognize his own", at the time of the massacre at Béziers in 1209. Now it has been more than one hundred years (it was precisely in 1866) since a scholar demonstrated, and without any difficulty, that that sentence could not have been uttered, since it is not found in any of the historical sources for that period but only in the *Dialogue on Miracles*

---

[3] "Executions of an almost medieval savagery", one such journalist wrote recently. Let us savor this "almost". Of course, in the century of concentration camps, cremation ovens, and the Gulag, how can we not be horrified by the savagery of a time when the portal of Reims or that of Amiens was sculpted!

(*Dialogus Miraculorum*), whose title gives a sufficient idea of what it is about, composed some sixty years after the events by the German monk Caesarius of Heisterbach, an author endowed with an ardent imagination and very little concern for historical authenticity. No historian since 1866, needless to say, has subscribed to the famous "Kill them all"; but story writers still use it, and that is enough to prove how slow scientific acquisitions are in this regard to penetrate the public domain.

Why this gap between science and common knowledge? How and under what circumstances was the gulf created? That is worth the effort to examine.

2

# CLUMSY AND AWKWARD

"The Renaissance was decadence", said Henri Matisse. The term Renaissance (*Rinascita*) was used for the first time by Vasari in the middle of the sixteenth century. He was saying exactly what he meant, what it still signifies for most people. "Arts and Letters, which appeared to have perished in the same shipwreck as Roman society, seemed to flourish again and, after ten centuries of shadows, to burn with a new brilliance." That is how it was put in 1872 by the *Dictionnaire général des lettres*,[1] one encyclopedia among many others at the end of the nineteenth century, by which one perceives perfectly the general opinion of the period and its level of education.

What are "reborn", then, in the sixteenth century are the classical arts and letters. In the vision, in the mentality of that time (and not only of the sixteenth century but of the three following centuries), there were two periods of light: antiquity and the Renaissance—the classical times. And, between the two, a "middle age"—an intermediary period, a uniform block, "crude centuries", "obscure times".

[1] Bachelet and Dezobry, published by Delagrave, 1872. The authors quoted were surrounded by a large collaborative group for the writing of their articles: the intelligentsia of the time.

To our period of structural analysis, it is not without interest to pause a little over the reasons that might have led to
this universal vision of our past. We are well situated to do
so, for the prestige of the classical times is largely dissipated
today. The last scraps did not withstand May 1968.[2] If some
confusion reigns today in calling classical values into question, that at the very least provides us with a profitable distance, a certain freedom of mind in their regard.

What characterized the Renaissance, then, was—as everyone agrees in recognizing—the rediscovery of antiquity.
Everything of any importance at that time in the world of
arts, letters, thought, manifests that same enthusiasm for the
ancient world. Let us recall that in Florence Lorenzo de Medici gave a banquet every year to celebrate Plato's birthday,
that Dante took Virgil as his guide to hell, that Erasmus honored Cicero as a saint. The movement had begun in Italy,
even before the fifteenth century; it spread into France, particularly during the following century, and won over more
or less the entire West, all of Europe. One need only mention the Florence of the Medicis, where all the monuments
are ornamented with pediments, columns, domes—just as
in ancient architecture—or the College of France, where all
the humanists were employed in studying ancient letters with
unequaled ardor, or the manifesto of La Pléiade, which proclaimed the necessity of enriching the French language by
drawing from Greek and Latin vocabulary.

Now if one examines precisely what this Renaissance of
ancient thought and expression consisted of, it appears, in
the first place, to refer only to a certain antiquity, that of
Pericles for Greece, and, for Rome, that which was inspired
by the century of Pericles. In short, classical thought and

---

[2] A widespread student revolt was staged in France in May 1968.—TRANS.

expression and those alone: the Romans of Caesar and Augustus, not the Etruscans; the Parthenon, but not Crete or Mycenes; architecture, from then on, was Vitruvius; sculpture, Praxiteles. We are simplifying, of course, but no more than those who use the word "renaissance". And everyone uses it.

It is even used for no reason at all. For with the progress of history, we have not failed to perceive that, in fact, Latin and even Greek authors were already well known in the Middle Ages. We know now that the contribution of the ancient world, classical or not, was far from being scorned or rejected at that time. Acquaintance with it was considered an essential element of knowledge. It is enough to recall that a mystical author like Bernard of Clairvaux himself skillfully wrote prose that was thoroughly nourished on ancient quotations and that, when he wanted to tease the vanity of a uniquely intellectual scholar, he did it by quoting an ancient author, Perseus; no one would dare assert that the latter was part of the general knowledge of any intellectual in more classical times.

In addition, scholars in our century have begun to use the term "renaissance" again. Noting that Latin and Greek authors were assiduously cultivated around Charlemagne, they have spoken of the "Carolingian Renaissance", and the term is commonly agreed upon. Others, still bolder, have spoken of the "Renaissance of the twelfth century", indeed, of "medieval humanism"—without too much success, it seems, in imposing either expression, which are rather jarring with respect to current usage. Thus we go from renaissance to renaissance, which cannot help but be suspect.

Upon consulting the sources of the time, whether texts or monuments, it turns out that what characterizes the Renaissance, that of the sixteenth century, and makes that period different from those that preceded it is that it poses in principle the *imitation* of the classical world. The knowledge of that world was already cultivated. How can we not recall here the importance that Ovid's *Ars amatoria* assumed in letters already in the eleventh century, or again, Aristotelian philosophy in the thinking of the thirteenth century. Mere good sense is enough to make us understand that the Renaissance could not have occurred if the ancient texts had not been preserved in manuscripts recopied during the medieval centuries. In order to explain this "rediscovery" of ancient authors, the pillage of Constantinople by the Turks in 1453 has often been evoked; this event would supposedly have had the consequence of bringing into Europe libraries of ancient authors preserved in Byzantium; but when one examines the facts, one sees that this had only a minuscule and not in the least determinative role to play. The library catalogues prior to the fifteenth century that have been preserved for us give abundant proof of this. To take one example, the library of Mont-Saint-Michel in the twelfth century contained texts of Cato, Plato's *Timaeus* (in Latin translation), various works by Aristotle and Cicero, extracts from Virgil and Horace . . .

What was new was the way classical antiquity was used, if one can put it so. Instead of seeing in it a treasure to be exploited (a treasure of wisdom, knowledge, artistic or literary process from which one could draw indefinitely), as had been the case previously, people suddenly realized that the ancient works could be considered as models to be imitated. The Ancients had achieved perfect works; they had attained Beauty itself. So, the better one imitated their works, the more certain one would be of attaining Beauty.

It seems difficult for us today to suppose that admiration must, in art, lead to a formal imitation of what one admires, to establish imitation as a law. Yet this is what happened in the sixteenth century. To express the admiration he felt toward the ancient philosophers, Bernard of Chartres, in the twelfth century, had exclaimed: "We are dwarfs who have climbed on the shoulders of giants." He nonetheless concluded that, thus carried by the Ancients, he could "see farther than they could".

But it was the very manner of seeing that changed during the Renaissance period. Dismissing even the idea of "seeing farther" than the Ancients, there was a refusal to consider them other than as models of all beauty, past, present, and future. A curious phenomenon, moreover, in the history of mankind: it took place at the time when immense unknown lands, other oceans, a new continent were being discovered. And yet at the same period, in France particularly, far from turning toward these new horizons, people turned back toward what was most ancient in the ancient world. And they imagined in all good faith that they were "discovering" an author like Vitruvius, for example, from whom they would draw the laws of classical architecture, although, as we know today, the manuscripts of Vitruvius were relatively numerous in medieval libraries and still today some fifty copies exist that predate the sixteenth century. But when people recopied Vitruvius in the Middle Ages, they studied the principles in his work without feeling any need to apply them exactly.[3]

Later on we will see the law of imitation expressed in the domain of letters. In what concerns architecture and the plastic

[3] Let us recall here the story told by Bertrand Gille, the historian of techniques. When, in 1525–1526, the Senate in Venice wanted to have a kind of boat built, adapted to battle against pirates, they disdained the plans of a master artisan in order to adopt with enthusiasm the design of a *quinquérème* copied from ancient models and presented by a humanist named Faustus (*Techniques et Civilisations*, vol. 2 [1953], nos. 5 and 6, p. 121).

arts, it is enough to note the division, which is very visible even today, between medieval monuments and those left us by the sixteenth century and classical times. There are scarcely any towns in France where one cannot see, often side by side, witnesses to these two periods, as well marked in their contrasts and their succession in time as archeological strata freed in the course of excavations. The simplest example is, in Paris, the contrast presented on two sides of the Seine: on one side, the Sainte-Chapelle and the towers of the Conciergerie; on the other, the courtyard of the Louvre. The division is as evident as that produced before the eyes of the Parisians when, in 1549, at the time King Henry II entered Paris, it was decided to do away with the *bateleiges*[4] of former times. That whole ensemble, both procession and the fair, which had formerly greeted the king in what had become his capital was sacrificed in order to substitute in its place decorations in the ancient style: columns, pediments, and Doric, Ionic, or Corinthian capitals on which only nymphs or satyrs resembling Greek or Roman statues were allowed to circle. The façade of the church of Saint-Étienne-du-Mont, which dates from this time, shows, in all its naïveté, the desire to copy faithfully the three ancient orders, crammed one on top of the next, while the Pantheon, from a later period, was a completely faithful reproduction of a classical temple.

What seems unjustifiable to us today is the very principle of imitation, the taste for the model, the copy. It was Colbert, instructing the young people he sent to Rome to learn fine arts to "copy exactly the ancient masterpieces without adding anything to them." One lived by this principle of

---

[4] The word comes from *bateleur* juggler, showman at the fair. The entrance of a king was the occasion of rejoicing for the common people.

imitation, in official circles at least, until a period very close to our own—in France especially, where classical culture has been considered the only form of culture up to our times. Let us recall that, still quite recently, one could not claim to be educated without knowing Latin and, indeed, Greek; and that, up to a date very near our own, the essential work of students of the fine arts in all areas, including architecture, consisted in drawing Greek and Roman plaster casts. Classical times have conceded artistic value only to certain works— which were not the best choices or the most authentic—of Chinese art, the object of a passing fad in the eighteenth century; or else, following the Napoleonic campaigns, to classical Egyptian art. Outside these two concessions to "exoticism", all Beauty was summed up, in architecture, in the Parthenon and, in sculpture, in the *Venus de Milo*.

Without taking anything away from the admiration aroused by the Parthenon and the *Venus de Milo*, what is surprising today is that such a narrowness of view could have been the law for some four centuries. Yet so it was: the classical vision imposed almost uniformly on the West admitted no other design, no other criterion than classical antiquity. Once again, the principle had been set down that perfect Beauty had been attained during the century of Pericles and that, consequently, the closer one came to the works of that time, the better one would attain Perfection.

In itself, if one admits definitions and models in art, this esthetic would be as valid as many others. There is no need to demonstrate, moreover, that it was so: it is enough to consider what it has left us, from the aristocratic dwellings on Île Saint-Louis in Paris to those of so many cities, such as Dijon, Montpellier, and Aix-en-Provence. What is strange is its exclusive and absolute character, producing as a consequence an anathema on the Middle Ages. All that was not in conformity with Greek or Latin modelling was mercilessly rejected. It was "the insipid taste of Gothic ornamentation" of which Molière speaks. "To the degree that the arts are brought to perfection," wrote one theoretician, the Abbé Laugier, in his *Observations sur l'architecture*, "there has been a desire in our Gothic churches to substitute for the ridiculous baubles that disfigure them some ornamentation of a more refined and purer taste." And, in the choir of the Saint-Germain-l'Auxerrois church, he was very pleased to see Gothic pillars "metamorphosed into fluted columns". The imitation of antiquity doomed to destruction the witnesses of "Gothic" times (after Rabelais, the term was used as if it meant "barbaric"). These works were too numerous, and it would have cost too much to destroy them all, so a great number have survived, for better or worse; but we know that a work was published in the seventeenth century to give useful guidance and counsel to those who wanted to destroy Gothic edifices, which, too often, in cities surveyed according to the taste of the time, detracted from the scene; it was necessary that all be rethought, ordered, corrected, according to the laws and rules that would render them conformed to Vitruvius or Vasari.

Some will most certainly cry out at this expression of the law of imitation; they will speak of simplism and will protest in the name of the triumphant genius, precisely through its genius, of the law of imitation and its corollaries, academic canons and so on. We will not take the trouble to refute these protestations. It would obviously be absurd to deny the beauty and grandeur of those monuments of the classical centuries that sprang from a will to imitate, which the genius of their authors knew how to assimilate effectively. And that absurdity would be all the more flagrant since it would only revive precisely that exclusivity that characterized the academic centuries. Is it not one of the benefits of history that we learn not to renew the errors of the past, in this case that narrowness of view that prevented an acceptance of anything not conformed to the esthetic of the moment, which is to say, that of antiquity?

This is because the history of art was drawn up during the time when this classical vision reigned uncontestably. It seemed at that time so normal to identify absolute Beauty with the works of antiquity, with the *Apollo Belvedere* or the Vatican *Augustus* that the works of the Middle Ages were quite naturally subjected to the same norms. As André Malraux wrote: "They judged in advance that the Gothic sculptor had wanted to sculpt a classical statue and that if he did not succeed in that, it was because he hadn't known how." And what is to be said of the Romanesque sculptor! He really would have liked to make statues like the *Victory of Samothrace*, but, most unfortunate at not being able to succeed in that, he had had to content himself, whether he liked it or not, with sculpting the capitals of Vézelay or the Moissac portals; he would so much have liked to make, according to the expression of one such art historian, "a true statue that one could inspect from every angle . . ."; he would so have liked to imitate the frieze of the Parthenon or the Trajan column . . . But no, in his "clumsiness" and his "awkwardness"—these are the two established terms used in my youth, and I am not sure they are not still used, at least in school, to describe the Romanesque artists—he succeeded only in surrounding the Christ of Autun with a breathtaking creation, in displaying the history of salvation on the royal portal of Chartres . . .

We are discussing only sculpture here, because painting—or let us rather say "color"—was such a horror to the classical centuries that they could think of no solution but to cover over the Romanesque or Gothic frescoes with plaster or to break the stained-glass windows and replace them with plain glass. This happened almost everywhere. We can consider that those at Chartres, Mans, Strasbourg, and Bourges, the only ones fortunately forgotten, allow us today some idea of how beautiful the color was at that period; the roses in the transept of Notre-Dame de Paris were preserved—except for the damage done during the revolutionary period—only because there was fear of not being able to remake them technically—which, just between us, was to render fine homage to the builders of the Middle Ages! The great art of classical times remained sculpture, sculpture in the round, of which, as it happens, there was very little in medieval centuries, and for all kinds of reasons, but particularly because there was then a preference to animate a surface rather than to execute an object in three dimensions. Another crucial question for the art historian of the Middle Ages has been: How were the sculptors able to "relearn" sculpting? The principle that sculpture had been a "forgotten" art was assumed as a given. Any time sculpture was tried, the attempts were "awkward, worthy of a child" (the term was one of disdain, not of admiration, as it would undoubtedly be today). Whence the value judgments made by art historians: a statue "of savage ugliness" (referring to the famous Sainte-Foy, the treasure of Conques), "very coarse illustrations" (referring to the famous Amiens Bible), "a frightful counterfeit of the human figure".[5]

The classical perspective has had another consequence, from which we are not yet free at the present time: the method that consists in studying in a work only the "origins", the "influences" from which it proceeds.

---

[5] We will not give references here: these quotations were extracted from books by historians otherwise full of merit, but endowed with more erudition than artistic sensibility.

It is of course understood that, since nothing is born of nothing, the study of sources and origins is indispensable in every discipline. But to reduce the history of art to the study of "influences" that might have led to such and such a form of art entails aberrant conclusions. The work of classical times appeals to the imitation of the ancient world; it refers to models; they were claimed, in any case. A sculptor could do himself glory for having perfectly observed the canons of Polycletes; a painter for having rigorously obeyed the laws of perspective. We know the wild enthusiasm of Leonardo da Vinci over the fact of having seen a dog bark at recognizing his master in a painting because the resemblance was so exact. And it is enough to have looked through that code of conventionalism, Diderot's *Essai sur la peinture,* to understand to what degree painting itself was conceived only in relation to a whole system of laws and references by which perfection was guaranteed: that is how he pronounces the laws of "historical landscape", those of "ordinary landscape", which would make the least informed reader shrug his shoulders today.

Using these same principles as the point of departure, a whole group of art historians have sweated blood and water to discover the origins and influences of the art of the Middle Ages, the sources on the basis of which imitation might have been carried out. For, in the end, it was very necessary that they imitated something, since art consisted in imitating either Nature or the ancient masters who themselves had imitated Nature. From which arose singular misunderstandings. In the eighteenth century no one doubted that all our Gothic art had been implanted by the Arabs! In the following century the history of art, which had become more scientific, nonetheless set the principle of imitation as the point of departure. But, since the distance between the work and the "model" was all too evident, they sought elsewhere. At the beginning of the twentieth century, the historian Strzygowsky entitled his work: *Orient ou Rome?* The question seemed staggering; today it seems almost rather naïve. Failing to find the required model in Rome, they sought it in the Orient, a term whose blissful vagueness at least enlarged the field of investigation. And they ended in flagrantly foolish observations like that commentary we have already had occasion to note with respect to a capital of the church of Saint-Andoche de Saulieu, showing stylized foliage: "Leaves of alder. Sacred tree of the Persians. Persian-Sassanid influence." The image of the little Burgundian sculptor striving to imitate the Sassanid Persians can sum up rather well the errors entailed in the attitude of art historians persisting obstinately in studying, not the works in themselves, in the society that had seen their birth, responding to its needs, to its mentality, but in the relations those works might have with supposed archetypes, which the historians went on seeking sometimes at a great distance.

In a parallel way, the classical vision led to an interest only in figurative scenes, those that at least represented something (awkwardly, it goes without saying). One could then rediscover the texts, identify the subjects evoked, establish relationships, bring out influences, practice at last for everyone the exercises necessary to the art historian according to the norms in use. Although Romanesque art may have presented a remarkable resistance to relationships and influences (and we understand that the Sorbonne rigorously insisted on this), tendencies of this kind still would have tainted even the rediscovery of medieval art by the Romantics, whose merits can never be overemphasized. Let us recall that it was as much to Victor Hugo as to Viollet-le-Duc that we owe the ability to contemplate Notre-Dame de Paris today. Nevertheless, in their period, the principle of imitation continued to reign, even if, unfortunately, it was the "Middle Ages" that were imitated, just as previously it had been antiquity. The result was the church of Sainte-Clotilde in Paris, a faithful copy of a Gothic cathedral—so faithful that it presented no special interest, any more than did the church of the Magdalen, a faithful copy of the Parthenon.

Now, the attention paid to the witnesses of "those times called obscure", in the artistic domain as in letters, leads one to grasp to what degree all art in the Middle Ages is invention—an invaluable witness, for it lays the foundation for the value and interest of efforts achieved much later, in a century of artistic revolution. Artists like Monet and Cézanne were much closer to the painters of Saint-Savin or Berzé-la-Ville than to Poussin or Greuze; artists like Matisse lived long enough to become aware of this: "If I had been familiar with them, it would have saved me twenty years of work", he said when leaving the first exposition of Romanesque frescoes given in France, shortly after the war of 1940. And it is very evident that the genius of a Matisse was expressed in entirely different ways than that of the Romanesque painters, but the knowledge of the Romanesque painters would have brought him precisely that inner freedom that he could not have gained except little by little, and in opposition to what he had been taught.

School discussions about "art-invention" or "art-imitation" are of course totally obsolete today. It was nevertheless necessary to mention these subjects, for up to and including our generation, they were of great importance, for they constituted the question of plastic or poetic expression. In feudal times a poet was called a *trouvère*, one who finds (*trouveur*, *trobador*), in other words: inventor. The term "to invent" (*inventer*) takes on its strong sense here, the one it assumes when we speak of one who finds a treasure (*inventeur*) or of the feast of the finding (*Invention*) of the Holy Cross. To invent is to put into play both imagination and research, and it is the beginning of all artistic or poetic creation. To today's generations, that seems obvious. Yet it remains a fact that for four hundred years, it was the contrary postulate that was asserted with a similar obviousness. One can hardly be surprised if a certain disorder is manifest in our times with respect to the forms in which invention, the capacity for creation, is expressed.

From this point of view, the study of the past can be very instructive: it is striking, in fact, that the lover of Romanesque art traveling around Europe and the Near East can discover everywhere the same types of architecture, the same semi-circular vaults supported by the same pillars, the same half-circle openings, in short, monuments all springing from the same inspiration. The same remarks could be made with respect to the Romanesque period as to more modern times, and the same criticism could be applied to it as is aroused by the tiresome uniformity of the "great ensembles" that are identical from one end of the five continents to the other.

It is enough to say that the study of Romanesque art could lead the creator of our times to wonder where invention is situated nowadays. In fact, we are witnessing today a search for originality that, in painting, for example, verges on frenzy, while, in a parallel way, the architect of the HLM[6] and other popular facilities renounces and abdicates, making of the city a universe of rabbit hutches at the very moment when, suddenly, young people become aware of the fact that man cannot live like a rabbit.

---

[6] The HLM manages and constructs public housing projects in France.—TRANS.

Would the formation of architects be responsible here? The architects of classical times and the teaching of architecture up to our own times considered external problems: the effect produced, the organization of façades, the regular alignment of buildings, the pediments, the decorations done in the style of the Ancients ... No one thought, in France particularly, to begin by examining what the needs of the users might be.

In a time when decisive progress was accomplished in the techniques of construction, the moment was not far off when it would be understood that one could do without the architect, that the essential problems of the building were those of the interior: problems involving the resistance of materials, the installation of pipes, access, passageways, interior layout, and so forth.

But the first great achievements of a truly modern architecture appeared very far from our country, in Finland, with Saarinen, in the United States, with Frank Lloyd Wright, and so on. For it was in France that the canons of classical architecture weighed most heavily and at greatest length on the formation of the architect. The only builder in our country who was resolutely innovative, or who at the very least adopted principles taking into consideration the person who was going to live in his buildings, was a foreigner, Le Corbusier, who was not under the influence of the school of fine arts.

Any effort today to maintain a place for the architect is totally artificial; the role for which he was prepared is no longer admissible; born with the classical times, he probably died with them; the wild imaginings in which some of them indulge represent scarcely anything but costly fantasies. The architects to whom the construction of a new basilica at Lourdes was confided at least had the humility to draw up in advance their acknowledgment of failure and to prefer a purely functional, and in any case subterranean, edifice (which was more useful). The contrast is surprising between this kind of admitted impotence in the domain of building and the unquestionable successes in other areas like roads, causeways, aviation: technical successes that are also, most often, aesthetical successes.

Would it not have been a crime to want first of all to "do the aesthetical"? Someone will certainly raise an objection here, citing the incontestable successes of those dwellings and hotels of the seventeenth and eighteen centuries, the mansions of the financiers or great government officials, not to mention Versailles. There is obviously no question of debating the point. They belong to an epoch and to conceptions that are obsolete today; they imply, besides, a taste for splendor and, even more, manual traditions on the part of the builders that have gradually faded over the course of time. The church of the Magdalen is very exactly in the line of the Palais-Bourbon; only the elegance has disappeared.

The comparison leads us to pose the question of art and luxury. The nineteenth century never doubted their interdependence for an instant. The indescribable Thiers, in defending the bourgeois, did not fail to bring out the fact that it was the rich who created the work of art through their generosity. The whole classical conception proved him right, but he was unable to account for the difference between art and the art object, and the result was his personal collection, a frightful junk collection of antique plaster casts and prize copies of Rome in Louis Philippe-style surroundings.

In the same period, those who experienced true artistic fervor saw themselves rejected by a society become decidedly incapable of discerning any artistic quality outside academic concepts. Whence the phenomenon that so profoundly marked the epoch and that made the history of art, at the end of the nineteenth century and beginning of the twentieth, a true martyrology: misery, madness, suicides; it is enough to evoke the names of Soutine, Gauguin, Modigliani, Van Gogh, and so forth. Artisans of a pictorial revolution who freed us from the classical vision, who were soon going to allow the greater number to *see* in a different way than according to academic canons, they were banished from a society fixed in its habits of mind; any feeling of admiration for their works, which seems natural to us, was at that time assessed as eccentricity. This attitude prevailed up to the moment when the French bourgeois suddenly realized that he had missed out on some excellent business and that art could also be a valuable commodity. Whence the opposite movement, which made a Gauguin, in a public auction, more costly than a Gothic cathedral,[7] but which actually was only a very marginal chapter of true art history. The generations to come (the movement has already begun) will undoubtedly be more than a little scandalized to note that ours led art into the lap of speculation, giving evidence even in this domain of the naïve confidence in numbers that seems to characterize our twentieth century; its glory will not be heightened by it.

And one might wonder if these young people who saw in the work of art a moment of ecstasy, a "happening", to be produced and destroyed at will once the emotion is past, were not, when all is said and done, closer to preclassical conceptions—apart from the fact, however, that they confused the *present* with the *instant*. Throughout the medieval

---

[7] A Gothic church in Senlis was put up for sale at the price of thirteen million old francs; paintings, during the same period, went for prices far beyond this value!

period, in fact, art was never cut off from its origins. We mean that it expressed the *Sacred*. And this link between art and the sacred stems from the very fibers of man in all civilizations; specialists in prehistorical times confirm this fact for us, and as early as the appearance of cave art.[8] All races, in all climates, have in their turn attested to this intimate communion, this inherent tendency in man that prompts him to express the sacred, the transcendent, in this second language constituted by art in all its forms. Thus each generation has had, across time and space, its own face, and the current facilities for travel and reproduction allow us to rediscover this face. Now it is very significant to note that the break, the falling off of artistic activity corresponds to the moment when, in the nineteenth century, a mercantilist conception of the "art object" appeared. And it is no less revealing that the "object of piety", a pitiable copy of the sacred for the use of shopkeepers, appeared in the same period. Still today it is striking to see to what degree artistic impotence is connected to the absence of the sacred. Certain countries, certain sects, certain churches, too, even certain religious edifices display their distance from the sacred in all its forms by their harsh artistic indigence. And that is not connected, as one might have thought even as late as the last century, to wealth or poverty. For there is a true poverty that is often magnificent: that of the painting in the catacombs, that of so many of our country churches. On the other hand, the original beauty of many of the edifices has been destroyed today by zealous priests, motivated by a laudable desire for poverty but confused about what is poor and what is merely squalid.

---

[8] We will content ourselves with referring to the work of André Leroi-Gourhan, among others, in *Préhistoire de l'art occidental* (Paris: Mazenod, 1965).

Perhaps it is in this direction that we must seek the secret of that capacity for creation that made of the least Romanesque capital, so similar in its lines to all the others, so obedient in its form to the general architecture of the edifice, a work of invention; a work of art so personal that the most faithful copy, the most precise casting, shouts treachery. Its functional character and technical utility, far from harming the artistic quality, are its almost obligatory supports; for art cannot be "added" to a useful object, contrary to what Ruskin and his school believed: it is born with it; it is the very spirit that animates, or else it does not exist. Such is at least what we learn from Gothic as well as Romanesque art, and this is a lesson our time is singularly prepared to admit.

To sum up the question as a whole, it is not an exaggeration to say that in the Romanesque epoch, as in the modern epoch, architecture was conceived according to norms that were similar almost everywhere, that there seems to have been a certain agreement, whether conscious or not, about basic measurements or units, according to more or less deliberate plans. The clearest example is that of abbeys, in which the construction of buildings is everywhere the same, responding to the necessities of life in common: chapel, dormitory, refectory, cloister, and chapter room, with variants that correspond to the modes of life of the different orders: the small houses of the Charterhouse, the barns and factories of the Cistercians, and so on. Undoubtedly architecture never responded more to common designs across a variety of populations; never was its functional character more strongly emphasized than with the construction of religious houses and fortresses; the necessities of the liturgy, in one case, and of defense, in the other, dictated the architectural forms.

Thus we see similar Romanesque edifices across all of Europe and the Near East. From the most humble—little country churches or Knights Templar chapels built on a simple rectangular plan with a semicircular apse marking the choir, even a *chevet plat*: that is the initial design, responding to the twofold necessity of a place of worship and a place of assembly—to the enormous pilgrimage church containing, around the choir, the ambulatory that allows circulation and onto which are grafted radiating chapels where traveling priests will say their Masses, the triple nave, which corresponds to the triple door, tribunes to accommodate crowds, and so forth. Just as the differentiation that would appear in Gothic architecture was born essentially of technical developments like the invention of intersecting ribs and that of the flying buttress. Just as the architecture of castles was linked to the evolution of siege tactics and to progress in weaponry.

How, then, does each edifice look so distinctive that it is absolutely impossible to confuse it with another of the same type? How is it that the abbey of Fontenay is so different from that of Thoronet, when in both instances we are dealing with Cistercian abbeys responding to the same original necessities, to the same traditional norms, to the same design? How can these nuances be so marked that we cannot confuse three sister abbeys belonging to the same region, like Thoronet, Silvacane, and Sénanque? In other places, the particularities could be explained by sculpture or ornament. But that, precisely in Cistercian churches, is almost nonexistent—which is again an imperative of function, since the absence of sculpture, color, and ornament is dictated by the desire for asceticism that characterizes the Cistercian reform.

Now, from one monument to another, what we have is a reinvention of Romanesque art. The builder knew how to place his creative sense at the service of necessary forms. Or better said: necessary functions, from which forms that are at once similar and endlessly new were born. It was a known fact at that time that man does not conceive of forms, properly speaking, but that he can imagine combinations of forms unendingly. Everything was for him a pretext for creation; everything that his vision could suggest to him became for him a theme for ornamentation.

For ornamentation is inseparable from the edifice and grows with it, in an almost organic harmony. Let us understand: this does not have to do with decoration or trimming, but rather this term expresses ornamentation in the sense in which the sword is the ornament of the knight, according to the example held up by the art historian Coomaraswamy.[9] By ornamentation we mean that necessary aspect of the useful work that moves or affects [*é-meut*]— which in the etymological sense signifies setting in motion. We know, then, that in everything man conceives, he must devote himself to conceiving it in splendor. Whence the time spent in sculpting a keystone or a capital, according to what the stonecutter's imagination would suggest to him— without, however, going beyond the place assigned to it in the edifice. Whence, too, the color that in the past enlivened the entire work, even a whole cathedral, outside as well as inside. Recent cleaning has permitted, as we know, a rediscovery of many traces of that painting that made an Armenian prelate visiting Paris at the end of the thirteenth century say that the façade of Notre-Dame resembled a beautiful illuminated manuscript page.

---

[9] In his very provocative study entitled *Why Exhibit Works of Art* (London: Luzac, 1943). A. K. Coomaraswamy, conservator of the medieval section of the Boston Museum in Massachusetts, exercised through his writings a certain influence on the painters of our time, Albert Gleizes in particular. The latter, as we know, was enraptured to discover Romanesque art at a time when the most complete scorn was displayed in its regard by those "with taste".

Ornamentation,[10] moreover, in Romanesque art especially, was dispensed only with an extreme economy, to con-
junctions of lines or volumes, to openings (windows, portals
. . .), to cornices. It makes one think of the ornamental se-
quences that at times intervene in plain chant, expressing as
they do an impulse that enriches the overall melody. Finally,
it is drawn from a few very simple themes.

I have shown, or tried to show, elsewhere the importance
of these themes of ornamentation, which are to plastic expression what the notes of the scale are to musical expression.[11] Several motifs, which are always the same even though
found in different civilizations, seem to have constituted something like a plastic alphabet of a time when one was in no way
concerned to represent nature, man, or everyday life as such
but when the most humble trait, the most modest touch of color
signified another reality, enlivening a useful surface by com-
municating to it some reflection of the beauty of the visible or
invisible universe. These motifs run through all Romanesque
creation, indefinitely revived, sometimes similar to each other,
like those chevrons or "pleated ribbons" that tirelessly accen-
tuated arches, sometimes developed to the point of giving birth
to aberrant vegetation and monstrous beings. The only rep-
resentations that retain the attention of the painter or sculptor
are those from the Bible, which is itself the most extensive rep-
ertoir of images that has been furnished to man, along with the
visible universe (both, Holy Scripture and creation, being at
that time considered "the two garments of the Divinity").

---

[10] It is fruitful to read, on this subject, the work of J. Baltrusaitis, *La Sty-
listique ornementale dans la sculpture romane* (Paris: E. Leroux, 1931), and also, of
course, the works of the brilliant H. Focillon, in particular *Art d'Occident* (Paris: A. Colin, 1938).

[11] *Sources et clés de l'art roman*, by R. Pernoud, M. Pernoud, and M.-M.
Davy (Paris: Berg International, 1974).

It was only just from the thirteenth century on that the vision changed and that, under the renewed influence of Aristotle, an aesthetic of forms and proportions developed.[12] So we can admire one by one all the Romanesque portals from Santiago de Compostela to Bamberg, or all the capitals gathered in the museum of the Augustines in Toulouse, or even clocks like those of Chapaize or Tournus, in order to try to grasp what marks these perfect works with such a strong singularity. But we can also, quite simply, illustrate this sense of ornamentation, always renewed on the basis of the same theme, with respect to a detail of everyday life that was very characteristic of a whole mentality: the hood. This was the usual headgear of the period. It goes back to the mists of time, since the medieval hood is nothing but the hooded cape of the Celts, our ancestors. This humble cape covering the head and shoulders gave birth to the "cowl" of the monks, but also to most of the headgear of men and women between the sixth and the fifteenth century. It has always and everywhere continued to be worn as a hooded cape, like those of the shepherds on the rood screen of Chartres or the peasants of Jean Bourdichon. But this same hood, placed so as to frame not only the face but the skull, while still composed of the same elements, is found continually renewed, whether by the material of which it is made (wool, velvet, satin) or by the way in which it is draped (the ends drawn forward, held in a turban, enlarged into a two-pointed hat . . .), so that it gives birth to all headgear, those still seen in frescoes, miniatures, and even in the Fouquet pictures. This hood, whose initial form has not changed but is ever

---

[12] See Edgar de Bruyne, *Études d'esthétique médiévale* (Bruges: De Tempel, 1946), 3 vols. Rijksuniversiteit te Gent, Werken uitgegeven door de Faculteit van de Wijsbegeerte en Letteren—97–99 Aflevering.

reinvented, is very characteristic of the man who wears it, both through its extreme simplicity and functional character and through that perpetual invention in which the personality of its possessor is expressed. Thus, whatever the period, the garment itself is the "theme of ornamentation"!

To come back to the history of art, it is enough to leaf through any manuscript whatever, even a simple charter of the time, to note the same capacity for creation: the perfection of the writing, the placement on the page, the seal that authenticates it, make us see firsthand what a perfect work can be. Perfect because it has truly been a creation. The one who made it is identified with his work; so much so that in his hand it became a masterpiece. We cannot sufficiently regret that most manuscripts remain unknown to the general public: what a profit there would be in making them better known by using modern methods of reproduction! One ornamented letter is enough to reveal what artistic creation could be in the Romanesque period. Let us not even speak of those that recount, for instance, an entire biblical or historical scene. A quite simple initial, in its essential, readable, recognizable form, is found taken up anew by every copyist, every illuminator, who made it his own and developed its inner possibilities, so to speak. It can be almost intoxicating; one becomes a veritable maze of foliage and interlacing, another gives birth to an animal that ends in a man's face, or a man becomes a monster or angel or demon; nevertheless, the letter has not been betrayed; it remains, but ceaselessly recreated. And this is without doubt what characterizes Romanesque art (and Gothic art as well, despite certain excesses that marked its end): respect for the essential function within a perpetual rediscovery of its inherent possibilities.

3

# CRUDE AND IGNORANT

In the sixteenth century, letters escaped the postulate of imitation no better than the arts did; there, too, it was necessary to conform to fixed rules of the Greco-Roman genre. A tragedy had necessarily to include the three unities of time, place, and action; any deviation was judged severely.

Moreover, it was as true in letters as in the arts that only the classical centuries of the ancient world were acknowledged: that of Pericles for Greek civilization, that of Augustus for Roman civilization. The study of language and letters in general was thus reduced, in fact, to one particular written expression, that of two or three centuries, which, as in sculpture, were made the models.

No other literary forms than those of antiquity: odes, elegies ... The sonnet had been tolerated insofar as this was an acquisition of the fifteenth century that had obtained its *lettres de noblesse* in Italy, a country venerated because of the ancient *Urbs*. A rigorous separation was maintained between genres: comedy, on the one hand; tragedy, on the other. And for the latter, which was judged to be "noble", it was obligatory to seek its subjects in antiquity. It must have cost Corneille to have written *Le Cid* and *Polyeucte*. And to have respected the sacrosanct "rule of the three unities" only at the price of truly incredible acrobatic feats in *Le Cid*. As for

Racine, more respectful of academic principles, his prefaces were expressly composed to excuse himself for slight violations of the law of imitation. In the better informed poetry, shepherds of Arcadia, nymphs, satyrs, and other fauns would evolve from then on, just as in the paintings of Poussin.

There had even been a question in the sixteenth century of reducing French verse to the rules of ancient prosody and metrics, based on a pattern of stress that actually does not exist in the French language. An imperative of such narrowness, taking so little account of the distinctive genius of the language, could not be maintained for long; on the other hand, child of the ancient hexameter, the Alexandrine was retained, imposing its tyranny up to the Romantic revolts and even much later still.

The imitation of classical Latin extended even to the study of the French language. There was an attempt to reduce the French sentence to the norms of the Latin sentence; whence the hair-raising rules of grammar and logical analysis that were imposed on students, with the "conjunctives of restriction" and other nonsense born in the heads of grammarians prompted by a somber pedantry. That, too, was the source of our spelling, one of the most eccentric there is. It was in order to imitate antiquity that the word *homme* was provided with an *h*, that *ph*'s were multiplied and *m*'s and *n*'s doubled . . . And thus was established the inevitable tendency (though it was rather belated, since it arose only in the nineteenth century) to judge the education of an individual by his spelling! Certainly the rule had been adopted at the same time as printing, which had imposed a certain fixity in usage. But this was a great misfortune for generations of schoolboys, who had to, and still have to, submit to this fantasy of Renaissance pedants, copied like all the rest from what ancient inscriptions dictated to them. We are witnessing today the shattering of this machine. There are some who are inconsolable about it. One can, however, wonder in what respect such a tendency, reactionary in its essence, was justified; it will seem to coming generations to be less and less justifiable. Let us repeat: the admiration one may feel for the ancient world is not in question here. In letters as well as in art—to adopt the classifications still in use—those in the Middle Ages had not ceased to draw from antiquity, without, however, considering its works to be archetypes, models. It was in the sixteenth century that the law of imitation, in this domain as well, was imposed.

Now, up until the present time, our academic programs have found a place only for classical literature,[1] that which begins in the sixteenth century. Is this intentional mutilation by which we are made to believe that letters and poetry did not exist in France before the sixteenth century admissible in fact or by right? We [in France] have fallen considerably behind today in knowledge of our own literary past, in contrast to other places such as Scandinavia, Germany, the United States, and German-speaking Switzerland. And this has been done through the whim of some academics and because a few generations of inspector generals decided to.

One very simple little fact seemed to me, a few years ago, to be significant on this subject: this was at the time when I was studying the letters of Héloïse and Abelard, around 1965. I had wanted, in the department of printed books in the Bibliothèque nationale, to verify the citation of Lucan's *Pharsalia* contained in the *Lettre à un ami*. Now, in searching through

---

[1] Let no one try to use as an objection the few scraps of medieval history or literature skimmed through here and there in the seventh or eighth grade. This could not be taken seriously.

the books on the open shelf, I noticed that there were no fewer than *six* copies of Lucan's *Pharsalia* at my disposal in the department of printed books: five different editions of the Latin text plus one translation. For a work that, let us recognize, is not necessarily a part of even an educated man's store of knowledge, this was a lot. The idea then occurred to me to see if I would find among the books on the open shelves a copy of *Tristan et Yseult*, or, indeed, any one of the works of Chrétien de Troyes. I looked for a long time . . .

The whole of classical antiquity, but not a single work from the period of our history that extends from the fifth century to the end of the fifteenth; this is not acceptable. Lucan's *Pharsalia*, but not *Tristan et Yseult*.[2]

On the other hand, several years earlier—in 1950, to be exact—during a stay in the United States, I had to write an article on Bertran de Born. I was in Detroit at the time; at the city's library, I found the work I needed all by myself, without the least trouble, right on the shelf, following the remarkable classification system that our libraries have since begun to adopt. What on the other side of the Atlantic is accessible to any reader is not available in Paris to the privileged reader (because in principle provided with university diplomas) at the Bibliothèque nationale. Nothing gives a better idea of the narrowness of our cultural conceptions, we who are so proud of our reputation as a people of *haute culture*.

[2]Another anecdote (1976): a translator wanting to refer to the work of André Le Chapelain, a theoretician of courtly love who lived in the circle of Eleanor of Aquitaine and her daughter Marie de Champagne in the twelfth century, made a naïve inquiry of a librarian at the Bibliothèque nationale; the latter referred her to the incunable edition of André Le Chapelain—an extremely rare work printed in the fifteenth century in Gothic script—unaware of the fact that this author has been published two other times, in 1892 and 1941; it is, however, true that the first publisher was Danish and the second, American . . .

Is it conceivable that there were a thousand years without any poetic or literary production worthy of that name? A thousand years lived by man without his having expressed anything beautiful, profound, or great about himself? Who could believe this? Yet we French, very intelligent people though we are, have been made to believe it, and for nearly four hundred years. All Boileau had to write was:

Villon was the first, in these uncouth centuries,
To disentangle the confused art of our old novelists

in order for the whole world to be convinced. Villon was the "first in date" of the French poets. That is found recorded in all the academic textbooks.

Now the thousand years in question saw the first appearance and development of the French epic (whoever said that the French did not have a "head for epics" was simply committing a historical as well as literary error); the invention of a new genre, that of the novel, which was unknown to classical antiquity; and finally the birth of the courtly lyric, which enriched the poetic treasury of humanity with a new strain.

This courtly lyric has been studied in its origins and its evolution by an eminent Zurich scholar of Romance languages, the author of *Origines et la formation de la tradition courtoise en Occident*, which the Sorbonne has carefully snubbed. It is not easy, nevertheless, to maintain a complete silence about a work such as this by Reto Bezzola, which is comprised of five quarto volumes published between 1949 and 1962,[3] filled with quotations and references that make it a kind of panoramic digest of the whole of lyric poetry up to the end of the twelfth century; it is beginning to be known here and there outside of university circles. The author unfolds

---

[3] Paris: Éd. Champion.

for us the evolution of medieval letters, first in Latin, then in the two languages, *oc* and *oïl*, of our Old French. In following this evolution, one is startled to note that this poetry, in its expression and in its development, is intimately linked with that of the arts in general. The first expression of this courtly lyric poetry is manifested at the end of the sixth century with Fortunatus,[4] who addresses to Radegund, the foundress of the monastery of Sainte-Croix in Poitiers, as well as the abbess Agnes, some Latin verse in which are already expressed sentiments dear to the poetry of the troubadours and trouvères of the twelfth century. This previously unknown inspiration derived essentially from a new regard with respect to women, henceforth addressed with a respectful tenderness. Thus, in this world described for us as a battlefield where barbarity confronts tyranny and vice versa is born this sentiment of extreme delicacy, which will make the woman, for all poets, a suzeraine.

One single writer has had the honor of surviving in our memories, the historian Gregory of Tours, whose name evokes for us the High Middle Ages; who leads us to liken all men of that time to the sons of Clovis, who, like many young people today, dreaded above all, as everyone knows, to have their hair cut; and all women to Queen Fredegund, whose favorite pastime, as everyone also knows, was attaching her rivals to the tail of a galloping horse. That allows us to label some three centuries as barbarous times, nothing more.

Yet, the same period of the High Middle Ages saw the book begin to spread in the form in which it still occurs today, the *codex*, the instrument of culture if there ever was one, which henceforth replaces the *volumen*, the ancient scroll;

----

[4] He would become the bishop of Poitiers.

printing would not have been able to render the services it did without this invention of the book.

It was also in this period that musical language was worked out that would be used everywhere in the West up to our times. In fact, there was intense poetical and musical activity at that time, with the creation of many hymns and liturgical chants, and it is known that plainchant, or Gregorian chant, long attributed to Pope Gregory the Great, dates from the seventh century. The very names of the notes of the scale were drawn from a hymn of the eighth century in honor of Saint John the Baptist, *Ut queant laxis*, by the Italian Guido d'Arezzo.

Only a few specialists are familiar with the great names that illustrate the field of letters during the High Middle Ages, but that does not mean they afford no interest. A little curiosity about the subject would permit one to recognize the flowering of an original spirit and astonishing capacities for invention in these authors, such as Virgil the Grammarian or Isidore of Seville in the sixth century, Aldhelm in the seventh, Bede the Venerable in the eighth.

Those who have studied these works, written in a difficult Latin, of course, but much less difficult for us than classical Latin, have appreciated their intense richness of thought and poetry, their striking freedom of expression.[5]

In letters as in the arts, it seems that the populations, liberated from the Roman yoke, spontaneously found once again the originality they had in reality never lost. The classical culture, which disappeared along with Roman education, magistracy, and, in short, command, was succeeded by a new culture that owed nothing to academic canons. Historians rarely resign themselves to discerning the Celtic vein in this culture,

---

[5] Let us refer here to the three volumes of *Esthétique médiévale*, the work already quoted by E. de Bruyne.

with its prodigious faculty for verbal and formal invention; yet, it seems to me difficult to deny, in Gaul and in Spain as well as in Ireland and Great Britain, the origin of that inspiration that everywhere gave rise to renewal: the taste for enigma, the play of words and assonances whose affinity is undeniable with that foliage, interlaced design, that lyrical profusion that one also finds in the art of the same period. The manuscripts in which the Celtic genius blossoms (notably those preserved in the libraries of Ireland) have something in common with the masterpieces of cloisonné jewelry one can still admire (if only in the collection of medallions in the Bibliothèque nationale, the Louvre, or the Cluny museum) and which, for lack of a better name, is called Merovingian in France and Visigothic in Spain. Some day we really will need to make up our minds to admit the common origin of these diverse forms of expression in the West of that time. There is certainly an ocean of prejudices to confront, a mountain of indifference to cross, but already we might judge that the decisive step has been taken; for it was indeed the classical formation, the classical perspective that, until a very recent period, prevented us from seeing in the works of the High Middle Ages anything but "crude and barbarous" productions.

Since we cannot dwell on these works, the study of which would require volumes, we will content ourselves here with pointing them out for those who might seek a thesis topic elsewhere than in the century of Pericles or with the emperors of Byzantium; here there is a practically unexplored source, which in our times might be greeted with a certain interest. We can, moreover, only bow before the admirable works of Pierre Riché,[6] which have been definitive and deserve to reach the largest audience.

---

[6] *Éducation et culture dans l'occident barbare* (Paris: Éd. du Seuil, 1962).

Another important study has been done on Isidore of Seville, who exercised a profound influence on medieval thought. His work, accomplished in Spain in the seventh century,[7] might be said to contain in germ the essence of the culture of the Romanesque and Gothic centuries. Now, his intuitions would merit the interest of avant-garde thinking; the principal work of Isidore of Seville, his *Etymologies*, is based on the potential meanings of each word in the language (outside of any philological concern, of course). Isidore of Seville, encyclopedic genius, unfolds in the exegesis of the word an extensive knowledge based on comparisons, indeed at times on a play of words, through which a whole synthesis is worked out that is at once scientific, poetic, and theological. The fact that he quotes innumerable ancient authors implies that he had their works at hand; this gives some idea of the immense learning of which Seville was the center in these High Middle Ages. These details are often forgotten when the translations of Aristotle subsequently done in Spain by the Arab philosophers are discussed: they could never have undertaken such a task in Seville, or elsewhere in Syria and other regions of the Near East, if they had not found there libraries that had preserved the works of Aristotle, and well before their invasion, that is, before the eighth century in Spain. Arab knowledge and thought could only draw from preexisting sources, from manuscripts that made this knowledge of Aristotle and of other ancient writers possible. It would be a perfect absurdity to suppose the contrary, as some have nevertheless not failed to do; the fault goes back to our scholarly textbooks, which mention Avicenna or Averroës but pass over Isidore of Seville in complete silence.

[7] Refer to the works of Jacques Fontaine, particularly *Isidore de Séville et la Culture classique dans l'Espagne wisigothique* (Bordeaux: Féret, 1959).

Jacques Fontaine has even remarked how, in architecture, the horseshoe arch, generally attributed to the Arabs, existed more than a century before their invasion into that "Visigothic" Spain they had so well studied.

* * *

Curiously enough, a kind of sharp check would be given to this momentum—felt at least in France and the Germanic countries—in the eighth and ninth centuries, effected, of course, by external events: the Arab invasions from the south (and let us not forget that their ravages extended up to Poitiers and Autun) and the Norman invasions to the north paralyzed life in a large part of our West. Provence, until late in the tenth century—972—lived in terror of "Saracen" raids; the bishop of Marseille could not reside in his diocese up to that date, and afterward the abbeys on the coast had, with difficulty, to rebuild their ruins and reconstitute their numbers.

But another factor intervened that, on the other hand, had an unarguably positive side: the restoration of the empire in the West. Taking over from the Roman Empire, Charlemagne, when he undertook to restore learning and culture, did it according to the Roman norms. He founded an academy; he provided us with a script for which we owe him a debt of gratitude, writing that he borrowed from Roman epigraphical characters. There was, under his impetus, what many academics, happily surprised, have described as the "first renaissance": an attempt to return to ancient forms. Had the empire survived, we would perhaps have known from that time on the civilization of classical inspiration that emerged in the sixteenth century.

In Charlemagne's circles, the lyrical vein, the study of language, the rather obscure endeavors by those poets called, for want of a better term, "hisperics", from the name of a collection that gathered them together, *Hisperica Famina*, gave way to a more reasoned literature in which a return to the ancient culture was attempted. The poets of this time celebrated glory, dazzling feats, and also friendship; but, as Bezzola remarks, "the love of a woman has no part in them." [8] They practiced a court poetry by adopting once again the ancient genres: idyll, elegy, epithalamium . . . and tried to revive classical letters. Charlemagne, who himself tried to revive the Roman Empire, founded, at Aix-la-Chapelle, the Palatine Academy, which gathered poets, grammarians, the learned, from all corners of that Europe which for a time was united under his powerful magisterium; they took evocative surnames: the poet Angilbert, a Frank, assumed the name of Homer, while the Visigoth Theodulf was called Pindar, and the Englishman Alcuin, Flaccus.

The arts of this same period, moreover, were also inspired by classical forms. They sought to resemble their models and nature, and some Carolingian manuscripts give us portraits quite as individualized as the Roman busts done under Augustus. Among the works of this period—notably the miniatures—it is not difficult to recognize the twofold source of inspiration: the original influence (Celtic interlacing, the exuberant foliage, the richness of the combination of forms) and the "controlled" aestheticism (columns with Corinthian capitals, concern for exactitude in landscape and perspective, respect for anatomy in the representation of people). Certain monastic centers like that of Saint Gall faithfully translated the efforts of the imperial reforms that were to revivify the ancient culture in its most classical expression. This reform is, moreover, interesting for us in that it calls on all the resources of the immense empire, and particularly on the

---

[8] *Les Origines et la formation de la tradition courtoise*, 1:91

monasteries of Ireland, those privileged centers of learning that were not affected by invasions. It is in Ireland that one finds the most learned grammarians of the time, and among them the best Hellenists.

Other tendencies existed, however, that this rather artificial resurgence of ancient academicism scarcely touched. We find an expression of it in a poem by Theodulf (*Pindar*); he describes the members of the Palatine Academy listening to a poem, whose form, in the style of Ovid, was approved by each as perfect; it was composed of distichs, whose learned versification was appreciated by all those present. All, with the exception of one, who was insensitive to such aesthetical delights; this was a Frankish warrior named Wibode. When, at the end of the poem, the audience poured out their acclamations, he lifted his hairy head, gave out some grunts that made the members of the illustrious Academy laugh, and finally, furious, left the room amid their teasing.

Might there not have been a comparison to make between this Wibode, the *membrosus heros*, as Theodulf calls him, the man of war left cold by the distichs inspired by Ovid, and so many young people (also long-haired!) who no longer want classical traditions; or even so many technicians who, knowing the value, interest, and often the urgency of technical developments, would find it vain and fastidious to be delayed by academic processes? Wibode at the Palatine Academy makes one think of an astronaut lost in the Académie des inscriptions.

Now, less than two hundred years after Charlemagne's death, the taste for letters was able to flower once again in the West, which had become more stable, at last delivered from invasions. And it was not an imitation of antiquity that was reborn but, indeed, the original Celtic inspiration, enriched by all that the various peoples had been able to bring to it. It was the Wibodes who triumphed and who were already working out a literature springing from their history and from their own genius, freed of all academicism and independent of "ancient influences".

The French-language epic was born in this eleventh century, spread by word of mouth and soon set down in a few manuscripts. The names of Roland and Olivier that we find on deeds of this time demonstrate that the *Chanson de Roland* had already spread by then, transmitted by minstrels and narrators. Commentators have worn themselves out seeking a "historical" origin for it; as ill luck would have it, a passage from Einhard seemed to prove them right, and so they struggled hard to see in the story of Roland the source of an epic whose subject is above all, precisely, epic: the work of imagination, a poetic construction, it appeals to a legendary Charlemagne only in order to raise, in contrast to the flight before Islam, whose theatre at that time was the Byzantine empire,[9] the lofty figure of the defender of Christianity, the protector of holy places, which, in this eleventh century, had been twice destroyed.

In other words, and Bezzola[10] has demonstrated this perfectly by relying on texts of that period, it is in the society of the eleventh century itself that one must seek the reason for and inspiration of the *Chanson de Roland*, just as of other epics, and not in a "historical source" to which the poets sought in any way to refer. The historians of literature have made the same error as the historians of art; they have transposed into the feudal period an imperative that was felt only

[9] Let us recall the battle of Mantzikert, which in 1071 literally freed Asia Minor from the Seljuk Turks.

[10] In his study entitled "De Roland à Raoul de Cambrai", in *Mélanges de philologie romane et de littérature médiévale offerts à Ernest Hoepffner* (Paris: Les Belles Lettres, 1949).

during the classical period: the obsessive concern in their works for origins and models (preferably ancient).

It is also in the society of the time that one must seek the source for the courtly lyric that blossomed again—after its eclipse—in Carolingian letters. It dawned at first in Latin, in the works of Baudri de Bourgueil, of Marbode, of so many unknown or unrecognized others. Then it blossomed in southern France, where the extraordinary poet William of Aquitaine, comte de Poitiers, would give it an incomparable inspiration, assuring its prestige down through the ages. In his wake, others, like Bernard de Ventadour and Jaufré Rudel, powerfully personal while cultivating a similar form of lyricism, expanded the full possibilities of a sentiment developed in the seignorial courts from which it would draw its name as courtly lyric. This is poetry profoundly connected to the feudal society, in which all relations are founded on the personal ties by which lord and vassal are reciprocally committed, promising the one protection, the other fidelity. The woman becomes "the lord" of the poet, the suzeraine; she demands fidelity; she arouses a love that also commands respect: *amor de lonh*, distant love, which creates a stirring tension between contrary feelings, and this is, paradoxically, the joy of the poet; to the Lady, he vows a kind of fervent, constant cult; she is all-powerful over him; the love that lives between them remains as a lofty secret that he could not betray, and it is by a *senhal*, a surname, that he designates her. It is, moreover, a characteristic of this period to make great use of emblems, of signs, of *senhals*; the coat of arms and armorial bearings that the knights carried on their shield, that any natural, moral person had engraved on his seal, were a part of this same tendency.

Some have wanted—and one wonders if ignorance is truly the only reason for it—to give to this courtly lyric sources

foreign to itself, to see in it, for example, the expression of a
"secret doctrine"—that of the Cathars, of course, the Cathar
having taken on epidemic proportions ever since the men of
the Sorbonne became aware of his existence. We are not
overemphasizing this point, as the error has been demonstrated, with a concern for historical truth that must be ap-
plauded in passing, by one of the most fervent supporters of
the Cathar cause, René Nelli.[11] To enter fully into the courtly
lyric, one must first of all know the period that saw its rise,
and most commentators do not.

It is expressed, not only in the *cansos* of the troubadours
and the songs of the trouvères, but also in chivalric novels.
The novel: one more invention of the feudal period, and
one that cannot be understood out of context. If most of the
characters come to us from the Celtic legends through the
brilliant work of Geoffrey of Monmouth, one still cannot
grasp *King Arthur, The Round Table*, or the *Quest for the Grail*
if one does not place oneself in the concrete life, the very
institutions of feudal times, and, to begin with, that of chivalry. They may be stories of fantasy, but all their details re-
mind us that they sprang from a society for which, first of
all, personal ties were important, a society that exalted the
ideal of the literate and courtly knight, one that idealized
fidelity to one's given word, and, finally, one that made su-
zeraines of women.

In retrospect, it is extraordinary that works so rich, of an
inspiration so original and of so dense a content, could be
passed over in silence like this, unknown by anyone, even
educators. For several years now, however, these works have
aroused an apparent interest: pocket editions of *Erec et Enide*

[11] *Les Troubadours*, Bibliothèque européenne, 2 vols. (Paris: Desclée de Brou-
wer, 1960–1966). Cf. the introductions of vol. 1, p. 9, and of vol. 2, p. 22.

and *Tristan and Isolde* have been published. Some authors have
been attracted by the person of Lancelot; a faculty of letters
created a chair of medieval iconography; another included
the *Quest for the Grail* in its program. But can one really draw
profit from these works and savor their poetic significance
without at least an elementary knowledge of the society that
gave birth to them?

\* \* \*

"The entrepreneurs as well as the players are ignorant people, mechanical artisans, knowing neither A nor B, who have
never been educated and who have neither eloquent speech
nor proper language nor the accents of decent pronuncia-
tion.... These illiterate people, with no understanding in
such affairs, of squalid conditions, like a carpenter, a consta-
ble, a tapestry maker, a fishmonger, have played the *Acts of
the Apostles*."

One must reflect a bit on these lines in order to understand
all that they contain. They are an excerpt from the parliamentary decrees that, in 1542, forbade the Confrères de la Passion
to continue playing at the Hôtel de Bourgogne, where they
were still producing medieval mystery plays for the common
people. The decrees were renewed in 1548, while still later, in
1615, the comedians of this same Hôtel de Bourgogne, bent
on the ruin of these Confrères de la Passion, who, for their part,
persisted in continuing their theatrical activity, declared: "This
*confrérie* has neither received nor produced anything but coarse
artisans, . . . who, in consequence, are incapable of public honor
or responsibilities and unworthy of the title of bourgeoisie,
through the reasoning of the Ancients, who made slaves walk
with the artisans."

We can see what is at issue here: the comedians of the
Hôtel de Bourgogne, who would end by having the estab-

lishment awarded to themselves for their own productions, aimed to destroy what remained of medieval theatre. Why? Because the latter was a matter of popular spectacle. And because the *confrérie* was not made up of professionals. Many causes are at work here: theatre people were tending, as in general were the masters of all professions, to form a corporation, or rather, to use the vocabulary of the period, a mastership or wardenship, which postulated the monopoly on the practice of a given craft in a given region. For, contrary to what was once believed and some still repeat, disregarding the results of a hundred years of scientific research, the golden age of the "corporation" (an eighteenth-century word) was not the thirteenth century, when it was encountered only as a complete exception in Paris, for example, but indeed the fifteenth and, above all, the sixteenth century![12] This was the case for the theatre people. For this reason we see them pursue the popular theatre with a veritable fury; to such an extent that at the Saint-Germain fair, the unfortunates who were playing pantomimes, seeing that they were forbidden to speak, began to sing! Some have seen that as the origin of the *Opéra comique*.

But it is good to appreciate in all their pungency the reasons enumerated in the parliamentary decrees: they testify that the Confrères de la Passion who were enacting the Acts of the Apostles or some Gospel scene or the ancient mystery plays were simple, humble: carpenters, tapestry makers, and so forth. These were "mechanical artisans"—those who practiced what were then called "mechanical arts", which is to say, handcrafts. Now these people, in the sixteenth century,

---

[12] And even where a corporation was not explicitly constituted, the example of the monopoly that was conferred on it gave rise to the search for similar monopolies.

no longer had a right to education; they had to "walk together with the slaves", for this had been the case in antiquity: a peremptory reason. And like all artistic forms, the theatre, a "noble" genre, could henceforward be the prerogative only of literate, educated minds, capable of appreciating the rule of the three unities and the separation of genres (which was unknown in the popular theatre!).

The comedians of the Hôtel de Bourgogne would achieve their end. We know that, having become the king's comedians, they would have the theatre monopoly bestowed on them by Louis XIV. That would permit Boileau, with superb ignorance, to write these lines of verse, which unfortunately everyone has remembered:

> The theatre, shunned by our devout ancestors,
> Was long an unknown pleasure in France.

In reality, what died with the Renaissance was this theatre that was still in touch with the masses, that called forth the crowds among whom it recruited actors and spectators. Yet, despite this persistent will to put an end to its tradition, this theatre was so lively that it survived even to our own time, here and there: when the artisans of the village of Oberammergau play the Passion, each in his traditional role, they are reviving the memory of an essential phenomenon of medieval life; to be ignorant of this is to be deprived of five centuries of extremely varied dramatic expression of which only the *Farce de maître Pathelin*, which is amusing but a bit brief, has been retained.

There were theatrical productions everywhere very early in the Middle Ages. We see it rise in a liturgical context: at an early period scenes from the Bible, especially from the Gospels, were dramatized. There is also mention made, in a text dating from 933, thus from the first half of the tenth

century, that, during Easter night, there was a dialogue between the angel and the holy women come to the tomb of
Christ—all undoubtedly represented by clerics or monks, who
played the scene as alternating dialogue. These paraliturgies
were then developed (Easter night, Christmas night, and so
forth), commemorating in general all the feasts of the year.
The theatre was thus linked to a sacred function, to a cel-
ebration through which the interior life was expressed.

But there was also an educational value, so the theatre was
in large part found in schools and universities. The statutes
of a Parisian college, that of Hubant, contain several illus-
trated pages describing the everyday life of the students. Now,
nearly half of these illustrations—like strip cartoons—show
them occupied with dramatic plays.

Our period has in large part rediscovered this role of the
theatre in life; cultural-life groups, even some business concerns, use theatrical activity, and there have even been ap-
plications of it in psychiatry or in various cases of mental
reeducation. We are obviously closer to the state of mind
that made the mystery plays spring up in the heart of medieval cities than to that which prohibited them. A master like
Gustave Cohen, moreover, understood the importance and
interest of this medieval theatre—and also understood that
one can study it only by playing it.

In any case, no one would argue today the importance for
the young, and even for those who are not so young, represented by this occasion for expression through word and
also through gesture. The word *geste* is, moreover, one of the
key words of the Middle Ages.

We should also recall the music with which all education
begins. We have seen how our civilization, from the musical
point of view, still remains indebted to the "obscure times"
that invented the scale! Leaving this subject to the specialists,

we will only dare to recall that an essential difference exists between music based on rhythm and music based on the measure, which, itself, was introduced only in the sixteenth century (it was "music measured to antiquity").

It does indeed seem that, from this point of view as well, we are actually closer to medieval times than to the period that saw the birth of "chamber music". In fact, whether vocal or instrumental, medieval music was perceived more as a "music of atmosphere" than as a spectacle, properly speaking. Up until the thirteenth century, moreover, there was no separation between musical language and poetic language: there was no poetry without melody; the poet was at the same time a musician. It is important to remember that at that time, if not everyone learned to read, everyone did learn to sing.

4

# TORPOR AND BARBARITY

In school textbooks, feudal lords are exclusively occupied with "trampling the golden harvest of the peasants". In journalistic style, they freely speak of "feudalism" with respect to financial corporations ("the great monetary feudalisms"), of authoritarian power, whether economic or political. During the revolutionary period, there was talk of abolishing "feudal laws".

The terms have been understood, according to the period, with very different implications. Thus, for historians of the nineteenth century, feudalism meant anarchy. At that time only centralized power was admitted, promulgating general laws applicable everywhere within national borders, following the same norms and within rigorously uniform administrative structures; it was in this sense that the 1789 Revolution put an end to what still remained of "feudal anarchy". Today such a historian would speak of the "system of feudalism". Now, if one refers to the most recent scholarly works, from Ganshof to Lucien Febvre, one notes that nothing is farther from any "system", nothing is more empirical than the feudal regime—with, besides, all the arbitrariness that comes from chance, everyday experience, usages, and customs. That said, nothing is less anarchical than the feudal society, which was, on the contrary, strongly hierarchical.

The study of that society would seem interesting, moreover, for more than one reason in a time when some [in France] demand "territory" if not autonomy, at least some capacity for autonomous development, when everyone feels the necessity of administrative divisions that are less compartmentalized than *départements* and more responsive to the profound native realities as diverse as those that constitute the soil of our country. It would not be irrelevant to recall today that a form of state different from those with which we are acquainted was able to exist, that relations between men were capable of being established on bases other than that of a centralized administration, that authority was able to reside elsewhere than in a city . . .

The feudal order, in fact, was very different from the monarchical order that replaced it and to which succeeded, in a still more centralized form, the order of state control that is found today in various European nations. If one wishes to understand what the term covers, it is best to examine its genesis.

\* \* \*

A centralized power in the extreme, that of the Roman Empire, collapsed in the course of the fifth century. In the disarray that followed, local powers arose; this was sometimes the head of a band of fellow adventurers grouped around him; sometimes, too, the master of an estate trying to assure for those around him as well as for himself a security no longer guaranteed by the state. In fact, the exchange of goods became difficult, the army being there more to maintain roads than to watch over the people; also, more than ever, land was the sole source of wealth. It was necessary to protect that land. Do we not see today the rise in certain countries of a parallel police force, in places where peaceful inhabitants consider themselves threatened by the increase in delinquency? This can help us understand what happened at that time: some little farmer, powerless by himself to assure his security and that of his family, applied to a powerful neighbor who had the possibility of maintaining armed men; the latter consented to protect the farmer in exchange for which the farmer would give him a part of his harvest. The one would benefit from a guarantee, the other, the lord, *senior*, the elder, the master to whom he had applied, would find himself more wealthy, more powerful, and thus all the more capable of exercising the protection expected of him. Finally, even as a stopgap measure imposed by difficult circumstances, the transaction, in principle, would benefit both parties involved. It was a man-to-man action, a mutual contract that higher authorities did not approve, and for good reason, but which was concluded under oath at a time when an oath, *sacramentum*, a sacred act, had a religious value.

Such was, in general, the scheme of relations that were created during the fifth and sixth centuries; of course the forms were very diverse according to the circumstances of time and place; they came to a definitive end in that state which one very rightly calls *feudal*. It was founded in fact on the *fief*, *feodum*. The term, Germanic or Celtic in origin, designates the right one enjoys over some material good, generally a piece of property: it was not a question of ownership, but, indeed, of use, a right to use.

Evolution moved more swiftly because of the mixing of populations that occurred during this period. The migratory movement referred to as the great invasions, in the fifth and sixth centuries, did not always have the appearance of violent conquest that one supposes; many peoples—let us think, for instance, of the Burgundians—settled themselves on the land as agricultural workers. A thousand years from now, with the distance of time, the historian who studies the twentieth century will not fail to see relationships with the High Middle Ages; is our century unfamiliar with migratory movements that give France, for instance, more than three and a half million workers who are Algerians, Moroccans, Spaniards, and Portuguese; do we not find Turks and Yugoslavians in Holland and Germany . . . ? The only difference stems from an ease of transportation unknown in the High Middle Ages. In consequence, once arranged, it was as a rule for life that the foreign worker settled with his wife and children on the farm that the so-called "Gallo-Roman" proprietor did not want to work.

Problems of course occurred as this movement progressed, problems that were resolved in a much more liberal way than one might be led to believe. Thus, the first question posed to someone who, arrested for a crime, appeared before a tribunal was: "What is your law?" In fact, he was judged according to *his* own law, not that of the region where he was found. Whence the extreme complexity of that feudal state and the diversity of customs instituted in them. To historians formed in Roman law, with its uniform and uniformly applicable foundations, this might seem the height of arbitrariness; during the period, the imbalances were certainly very great from one region to another, but, there, too, we are closer to these concepts now, since we understand better today that justice and truth consist in judging each according to his own law.

However that might be, it was a different order from the imperial order that was instituted during those centuries considered the darkest of the dark ages—those from approximately the fall of the Roman Empire (fifth century) to the restoration of the Western empire by Charlemagne three hundred years later. In this period and despite the misadventures, the most important of which was the great shock brought to all the known world by the irruption of Islam—the "Saracen terror" often referred to on deeds—the feudal order replaced the old imperial order everywhere in Europe. The authority that Charlemagne sought to restore could do scarcely more than sanction an established fact: which is to say that the power formerly concentrated in a precise place, the expression of a determined will, no longer existed. Only local powers reigned; what was referred to as public power was fragmented and spread into a multitude of cells that could be called independent if that term did not signify for us the faculty of acting according to individual whim. Now, in fact, all individual will was limited and determined by what was the great force of the feudal age: *custom*. We will never understand what that society was if we fail to understand custom, which is to say, that collection of usages born of concrete acts and drawing their power from the times that hallowed them; its dynamic was that of tradition: a given, but a living given, not fixed, ever susceptible to change without ever being submitted to a particular will.[1]

It was not so very long ago that one could observe the survival of such customs in English-speaking countries, for example. Thus, to keep to one small, very humble act of everyday life, when foreigners in London, before the war, were surprised to see sidewalks covered with chalk drawings (a practice that has since spread nearly everywhere) and when

---

[1] I once found this pearl in a study coming from an *agrégé* [one who has passed the competitive examination for posts on the teaching staff of lycées and universities] in history: "In the Middle Ages, the laws were called customs." One understands nothing about the period if one does not grasp the difference between a law, issuing from a central power and by nature fixed and defined, and custom, a collection of usages born of the soil and constantly in evolution.

they asked why, in streets with dense traffic, this practice was not forbidden (a simple decree from the minister of the interior or the prefecture of police would have sufficed here in France), they were told that this was not possible: since the first ones to devote themselves to this kind of popular art (or, if you prefer, begging in disguise) were allowed to do it over a rather long period of time, it was no longer possible to retreat from that tolerance.

This is what occasioned medieval custom: usages were introduced under the pressure of circumstances; some of them fell into disuse; others were immediately fought, others in the end were accepted or merely tolerated by the group as a whole and soon acquired the force of *custom*. It was thus that rents, for example, were very early fixed in very diverse ways according to domain. Now, once accepted on both sides and collected for a certain time, there could no longer be a question of abolishing them: it was necessary to wait for them to disappear of themselves. Custom, usage that was lived and tacitly approved, governed the life of the human group and constituted obstacles to individual caprices. Of course there were always individuals who tried to jump over the obstacles that the group or society set up, but then the matter fell into the category of an infraction, such as a delinquent does today; and if no public power to sanction offenders existed, the latter were rejected by the group, which amounted to the same thing, especially in a time when life was difficult for an isolated person.

Such were the bases, very briefly outlined, of this feudal society, radically different from what has been known since then with respect to social forms. Thus the right of private war was allowed, which was the right for the group to avenge an offence suffered by one of its members and to obtain reparation. Also, when we think of feudal society, we must acquire the habit of thinking of lineage, family, household, rather than of individual voices. Yet this same society rested on personal connections, of man to man; one committed oneself to a particular lord. If some incident occurred, it was necessary to renew the agreement that had been made. In this way the history of feudal times unfolded, made up of games of alliances that were formed and then dissolved; here, it was a vassal—a word of Celtic origin, we should note in passing—who swore homage to his lord, but who then proved guilty of infidelity; there it was another who, having sworn homage to the father, refused to do as much for the son . . . Feudal wars, which in no way resembled modern wars, drew their origin from that extremely complex fabric of personal agreements and community traditions that constituted the society of that time. In our own time, when we see occasional community-oriented trends develop, in reaction to the impersonal power of the law and to the even more impersonal power of the collectivity, it would be very interesting to study this "precedent"; not with any thought of imitation, certainly, but simply through historical and human curiosity. This might allow us, among other things, to sweep away the reproach of utopianism always leveled against new attempts.

A society with communitarian leanings, although administered by personal agreements, the feudal society was also essentially a country, rural society. We have been so dominated by forms of urban supremacy that we admit as an axiom that civilization comes from the city. Even the word "urbanity" is a relic of the ancient *urbs*. But this is not a medieval term. The entire history of feudal times proves the contrary for us.

There was a civilization born of the castle, which is to say, of the domain, then, springing from a rural framework, having nothing to do with urban life. This civilization gave birth to the courtly life whose very name indicates its origin, for it was born of the *court*, the courtyard, that is, the part of the castle where everyone met.

The feudal castle: an organ of defense, a vital place of the domain, the natural sanctuary of the whole rural population in case of attack, the cultural center, rich with original traditions, disengaged from any ancient influence (although everything bequeathed by antiquity was often known and studied: did not one monk on his way to Montreuil-Bellay find a lord absorbed in reading Vegetius?). It is very significant that the terms courtly and courtliness were attached to this culture; they sprang from a civilization that owed nothing to the city and evoke what was proposed at that time as the ideal for an entire society: a code of honor, a kind of social ritual, which were those of chivalry; a certain freedom of manners, too; and finally a respectful attention demanded of men by women.[2]

The castle was not the only place to assume an educative function: monasteries, which were also spread over the countryside, were centers of study as well as of prayer; one need only look at the abundance and quality of the manuscripts in the Mont-Saint-Michel library for proof; in spite of its isolated position, battered by the sea, on a small, sunken island (which, at the end of the Middle Ages, would be made a prison at least as often as a convent), this monastery was, like all the others of the period, a center of learning in the rural setting, in close relations with the neighboring population.

---

[2] Later, in classical times, the term "court" would be reserved for the royal entourage. It is interesting to think that it would at that time give birth to the words "courtesan" and *courtisane* [meaning flattering or obsequious]—both far removed from courteousness. One etymology, two civilizations.

The monks, especially the Cistercians, generally worked one part of their land themselves, but they also had tenant farmers, serfs or free men; examples of serfs who attained high ecclesiastical or lay positions show, moreover, that the religious communities did not consider peasants to be a convenient reserve labor force or source of lay brothers. From the beginning of the thirteenth century, we see the creation, in the middle of towns, of a new type of monastery that would profoundly mark the general evolution. If Dominican or Franciscan brothers settled in an urban area, it was a sign that the towns had assumed some importance; but much more time would pass before this phenomenon developed to the point of supplanting the influence of Benedictine monasteries, centers, like the castles, of a truly landed, rural, domanial culture. Little by little we will see this culture decline; by the sixteenth century, it was in the town that we find the organs of government and administration, the schools, in a word, the centers of learning and power; just as in the seventeenth century, despite the very clear-sighted efforts of some, like Sully, there would no longer be any intellectual activity in the rural milieu, except to a very weakened degree—this degeneration soon extending to the province as a whole,[3] all those judged worthy of a true life of the mind were to be found in Paris, where the University and the College of France were located, or at court. The definitive end was reached with the administrative reorganization of France in 1789, making the principal city of each *département* the center of all administrative activity and Paris the head that was in charge of all. Paris, from the eighteenth century on, was the capital

---

[3] One need only think a bit about a comedy like *Monsieur de Pourceaugnac* to understand with what scorn the "province" was from then on overwhelmed through that attentive servant of the court named Molière.

of all learning in France; in the nineteenth century, it was the culmination, the career high point for state functionaries and practically the only place where all that makes a civilization worthy of the name was assembled.

As oversimplified as this picture may be, it seems scarcely debatable. What is debated today, on the other hand, is the validity of such a supremacy, of a centralization that thus brings to one unique place, not only all the organs of government, but even the means of acquiring higher instruction and formation.

It is a healthy reaction that urges decentralization today. When we think that certain domains, as in the example of theatrical expression already cited, or like dance or singing, were, not so very long ago the nearly exclusive prerogative not only of cities in general but, in France, of Paris and its conservatories—one can only be astonished; the monopoly created in the seventeenth century for the use of the king's comedians, and strongly emphasized after that, has been shown to be truly oppressive, cutting short any valid activity in the provinces and in our countryside.

One can, moreover, wonder if that situation would not have been even more prolonged if it had not been for modern technological means: radio and television have ended in allowing everyone to benefit from what had been reserved for a few. The diffusion of culture is facilitated by it today; one can criticize the level to which that culture has dropped, but it remains true that the former monopolies have ceased to exist and that, contrary to what one might have believed, radio and television give rise nearly everywhere to local activities: music, dance, and theatre blossom unexpectedly even in regions once called "very remote" and become once again a common domain, accessible to everyone. This immense progress is almost universal and is accompanied everywhere by entirely local attempts to re-discover the original sources of culture, local sources, those of the village, of the region, which have been unrecog-nized, disregarded, for so long, but which, when all is said and done, ask merely to spring up once again. Moreover, by expanding our reflection from France to Europe, from Europe to the entire world, it is probable that this new sensibility will develop, taking into consideration both this world dimension and these many local opportunities in which each human group, tribe, ethnic group, or community what-ever, indeed, each human being, can feel rooted and can express himself.

But to return to our subject, we still need to examine the role that the king played in feudal society and particu-larly at the time when that society achieved its equilibrium and its high point, which is to say, from the end of the tenth up to the fifteenth century. The expression about kings "who in a thousand years made France",[4] seldom used to-day, created an illusion about an important point: the con-fusion between medieval royalty and classical monarchy. It does not matter whether there was or was not hereditary continuity;[5] if we consider royalty with respect to its polit-ical, military, administrative role, how can we see in Louis XIV the successor of Saint Louis? That the terms are the same is, then, in itself, a historical error; in reality, the evo-lution of the royal function has been so profound that the use of different terminology should be imperative. The feu-dal king was one lord among other lords; like the others,

---

[4] It was, as we recall, that of Maurras and *l'Action française*.

[5] The notion of a legitimate king, tied juridically to the custom of trans-mission from father to son, was important for peoples in the past; it does no one any harm to observe that it is no longer of any consequence today, and has not been for quite a long time.

he administered a personal fief, in which he rendered justice, defended those who populated his domain, and collected rent in kind or in money. Beyond this domain, there
was the king, the one who had been marked by holy oil;
he was the designated arbiter in conflicts, the suzerain of
suzerains, the one who assumed the defense of the kingdom and to whom, for that reason, the other lords owed
military aid, fixed, moreover, for a very limited time: forty
days per year. Custom ruled the methods by which this aid
was furnished to him, but his title of king did not signify
that his economic or military power was greater than that
of some particular vassal; human prudence simply dictated
to him the concern to maintain a balance either between
the great vassals or between the latter and himself; and this
is why marriages and inheritances represented so great an
importance at that time.

Let us note, moreover, that if the royal power was above
all moral, it was not for all that Platonic. One fact after
another demonstrates this: when the king of France Louis
VII wanted to fulfill his duty of protection with regard to
one of his more powerful vassals, Raymond V, count of
Toulouse, threatened by Henry II Plantagenet, his presence
alone in the castle of Toulouse was enough to make the
aggressor abandon his bellicose plans. This happened in 1159.
Languedoc, which had been part of the kingdom of France
from the most distant times, thus furnishes a striking example of relations between suzerain and vassal during the
feudal period. In our time, historians have tried hard to
find various reasons, plausible to their minds (that is, of the
economic or military order), to explain Henry II's attitude
in giving up the siege of Toulouse for the sole reason that
his suzerain, the king of France, was enclosed there; but
contemporaries themselves understood perfectly that Henry

Plantagenet, a king himself,[6] had to respect what was for the feudal king the rules of the game; in his own domain, he did business with vassals who, if he had violated those rules, would not have failed to take this as a pretext for acting similarly. The episode is very significant, and, also, the lack of understanding to which it has given rise.

Whatever his authority might have been, the feudal king possessed none of the attributes recognized as those of a sovereign power; he could neither decree general laws nor collect taxes on the whole of his kingdom nor levy an army. But the evolution about to begin, notably in the fifteenth century, ended precisely in conferring these powers on him; it was the direct consequence of the renaissance of Roman law, to which it would be impossible to impute too much importance. It was southern jurists, all powerful in the court of Philip the Fair, who were the first to formulate the principles that would make the suzerain a sovereign: "The king of France is emperor in his kingdom . . . his will has the force of law"—such principles, at the time they were proclaimed, were purely utopian; but nothing is more common in world history than to see utopias become realities. In this case, some two hundred years were necessary. The evolution would probably have been less rapid if circumstances had not accelerated its progress. The wars and great public disasters, famines, epidemics, and so on, that marked the fourteenth century and the first half of the fifteenth were determining factors. Charles VII would be the first king to arrange, at the end of his reign, for an army and for permanent taxes. His son Louis XI inaugurated the positioning of a truly centralized

---

[6] Henry Plantagenet, vassal of the king of France for his continental fiefs (in practical terms, the western part of the country, from Normandy to Gascogne), was also, after 1154, king of England.

administration that would have fulfilled the wishes of Philip the Fair. But the king would truly become a monarch, possessing full sovereign power, only with Francis I, when the latter concluded with Pope Leo X the Concordat that made him head of the Church of France, with powers to name the bishops and abbots of his kingdom; the Church was to be profoundly and fundamentally transformed by this. The monarch, the one who governed *alone* (*monos*), possessed full powers, not only over the administration, army, and finances, but even over consciences. From then on the term monarch, not king, was appropriate. The power, particularly in France, was absolute, centralized; certain inconsistencies, nevertheless, limited his power: thus the old institutions—those, precisely, from feudal times—had to be reshaped. For failing to have undertaken this, certain sectors—for example, that of finances or the army—would constantly find themselves in an unstable position in the French monarchy.

The resources of the monarchy would remain more or less confused with its patrimonial resources, those of the former royal domain; nothing less than the Revolution would be required for the state really to arrange a system of public finances worthy of that name. The army would remain composed of volunteers, recruited with difficulty, and its manpower was sufficient only thanks to the appointment of Swiss battalions, which, in three centuries, have furnished France with more than a million soldiers and four hundred generals. Finally, the monarchs, as "absolute" as they were, did not intervene in private law, contenting themselves with regulating, when need be, the form of the acts within the jurisdiction of private law; local customs thus continued, in essence, to govern this law up to the time of the Revolution.

What is strange is that there was talk at that time, in 1789, of abolishing "feudalism". The expression was as inaccurate as it could be, the rule of the country having considerably evolved in some four hundred years. As Albert Soboul writes, "Feudalism, in the medieval sense of the word, no longer corresponded to anything in 1789"; but, he adds, "for contemporaries, for the bourgeois, and even more for the peasants, this abstract term covered a reality they knew very well (feudal laws, seignorial authority) and which was finally swept aside." [7]

The terms "feudal" and "feudalism" were at that time, in fact, unfortunately compromised. Just as one calls "Gothic", with a strongly pejorative shading, everything that is not "classical", so they called "feudal" everything of the Ancien Régime no longer wanted. In this "everything", there were a few distant survivals from "feudal" times: for example, the very presence of castles—those at least that had escaped the methodical destruction of Richelieu and Vauban (simple neglect, most of the time!); or honorary privileges, like that of presenting the blessed bread to the parish church for certain feasts; or again, more rarely, some remnants of seignorial justice, with regard to which legends never failed to circulate that nearly always sprang from wordplay, like the all-too-famous *jus primae noctis*, and so on.

The ambiguity of certain terms sometimes, quite wrongly, evoked the Middle Ages—for example, that royal forced labor, instituted in 1720, which weighed heavily on the peasant class but which had nothing to do with the old seignorial forced labor, which had nearly everywhere been replaced or fallen into disuse.

What was more serious and added to the confusion was the fact that the bourgeois proprietors who had bought the land during the three centuries of the Ancien Régime had

[7] *Aujourd'hui l'histoire* (Paris: Éd. sociales, 1974), 271.

worked ceaselessly to seek out extensions of the old rights (various rents in money or in kind) to which the lands had been submitted in the past, in order to collect them again. It is pointless to add that they did not seek to assure the other party of protection, which had become the duty of the central power. In the eighteenth century, a mastership (corporation) grouped together those who were called feudalists, researchers connected with this task, which examined the old cartularies and set up *censiers* and *terriers*.[8]

If there were ever an exploitation of the peasant, of the man of the earth, it was indeed during this period. The search for ancient rights called "feudal" reestablished the taxes that had fallen into disuse when the land was purchased, either because the old lords had stopped collecting them for so long a time that custom confirmed their abandonment (that was what happened, for example, during the crusades, from which many did not return), or again when they were "redeemed" or "subscribed"[9] by the peasants.

Now, the search for ancient rights by the bourgeois who had become owners of formerly seignorial domains was instituted under such conditions, with the support of the *parlements*, that it was up to the peasant to supply proof of this "redemption"—which was for the most part impossible, since the agreements were more often verbal than written during the feudal period. Finally, the rights thus restored were added together, although they had often been made only to succeed each other in actual fact. The desperate eagerness that set the peasants, during the Great Fear in 1789, to burning

---

[8] Registers from which these ancient rights were picked up; it is always surprising to note the great number of these *censiers* (taken from *cens*, which were the taxes owing on the land) dating from the twelfth and thirteenth century, in public or private archives.

[9] Replaced by a periodic tax (generally an annual one).

the seignorial archives is therefore quite understandable. But these rights were "feudal" in name only. The tithe is a typical example of the reappearance of these taxes. Levied as early as the High Middle Ages in certain regions, extended to most rural goods during the Carolingian period in order to provide for the needs of clerics, it ended by becoming part of the charges attached to a piece of land: if the latter was purchased by a bourgeois, he continued to collect it even if he did not provide—and with good reason—the service at the altar one would expect from a priest. In how many localities, under the Ancien Régime, did the ecclesiastical tithe follow this mutation? We do not know with any accuracy, but the act must have been rather widespread, since the term "bourgeois tithe" had become common by the eve of the Revolution.

The ambiguity of the term "feudal" was complete by the same period. As, also, that of the term "Gothic" was complete—or as the ambiguity continues even today with the term "Middle Ages"; for it is perfectly absurd to designate by the word "middle", as if it were a mere intermediary period, a period of a thousand years of human history.

This must be emphasized because of the errors and misuse to which this term feudalism has given rise, particularly when it has been set in opposition to that other term "bourgeoisic", itself just as ambiguous. Marx's *Manifesto*, published in 1847, reflects the state of historical science of the period. It fixes the thirteenth century as the beginning of the "battle against feudal absolutism" and attributes to the bourgeoisie "an essentially revolutionary role" in history. Did the bourgeoisie not uproot the countryside from a "state of torpor and latent barbarism"? These are all propositions that are today [1977] unacceptable for the historian; those who continue[10] to perpetuate such errors of vocabulary, which are intellectually necessary if one wants to maintain at any price the feudalism-bourgeoisie-proletariat, prolong an ambiguity just as erroneous as the continued use of the term "Gothic" during the era of Marx. In other words, the Marxist historians, who speak of feudalism destroyed by the French Revolution, make one think of those ecclesiastics who see in the Second Vatican Council the "end of the Constantinian period"—as if nothing had happened, in more than sixteen hundred years, between Constantine and Vatican II, as if the beginning of the sixteenth century, particularly, had not led to that radical change in the state of the Church that was (without any play on words) the establishment of the Church of state.

* * *

If one wants to stick to historical facts and not justify a priori ideas, it is indeed necessary to recognize that the birth and expansion of the bourgeoisie coincide exactly in time with the great expansion of the feudal system. It was in the first years of the eleventh century that the word "bourgeois" itself appeared in texts; and it was during the actual feudal period

---

[10] Let us cite, among many others, the Soviet historian who saw in Peter Abelard "a champion of the independence of cities", as opposed to Saint Bernard, who was supposedly a "defender of feudalism"! It would take a clever man to find in Abelard's writings the least allusion to any preoccupation whatever with regard to the independence of cities, or, on the other hand, in those of Saint Bernard the slightest concern with "feudalism"! Both came in a similar way from the minor rural nobility (which was of very little importance to them, since from their youth they had both surrendered their rights); they had in common what constituted their sole interest throughout their entire existence: the heavenly City, the kingdom of God—however different the paths they may have chosen to approach it.

Moreover, it is enough to recall here the famous controversies with respect to Mendel and Lyssenko to note that science—and history is a science—cannot adapt itself to preestablished systems.

(eleventh-twelfth-thirteenth century) that the creation of new towns, the establishment of rural districts, the compilation by towns of their statutes, and so on, took place. If there were "class wars", they were produced precisely within and in the very heart of that bourgeoisie of the towns, where a certain number of tradesmen, more ambitious and clever than the others, occasionally overturned the restrictions against monopolies and anything that led to excessive profits. These internal battles, moreover, ended, in most cases, in costing the towns their autonomy, and did so at the very moment (between the very end of the thirteenth and the end of the fifteenth century) when the quasi-autonomy of the seignorial domain was also weakening. In France, the great victor was the king; he became a monarch at the beginning of the sixteenth century, at the time when, almost everywhere in the West, nations were being constituted in which the state, the public power, regained the importance it had had in Roman antiquity. In assuming power at the time of the Revolution, the bourgeoisie destroyed, not "feudalism", but the Ancien Régime that it had largely contributed to creating but which kept it out of political power.

Of course, by setting one schema against another in this way, we must calculate what irreverence, almost sacrilege, there is in taking such liberties with dogmas; perhaps the historians of future ages will be surprised to see this status of dogma accorded indiscriminately by most of the intellectuals of our time to everything coming from German philosophy: Marx, Nietzsche, Freud, and so many others.

Nevertheless, to confine ourselves to our subject, we cannot do less than note the inconsistency of Marxist historians who claim to base themselves on history but deny to the latter the right to have made any progress in the course of some one hundred and fifty years.

After all, we are no longer in the era of Galileo ...

# 5

# OF FROGS AND MEN

Slavery is probably the one thing about civilization that most profoundly marks ancient societies. Now it is curious, when one glances through history textbooks, to note the discretion with which this is brought up; whether it is a question of the disappearance of slavery at the very beginning of the High Middle Ages or of its abrupt reappearance at the beginning of the sixteenth century, one witnesses a rare restraint on this subject. If one amuses oneself, as I have done, by going through school textbooks for high school classes, one observes that *none* of them points out the progressive disappearance of slavery from the fourth century on. They mention medieval serfdom in very severe terms but pass over in silence the rather paradoxical return of slavery in the sixteenth century.

For a simple mind, there is something surprising about that; it seems difficult to deny that ancient society considered slavery to be natural and necessary. If in the course of the later years of this society (which, moreover, corresponded with the rise of Christianity) Seneca pointed out that a slave is a man (a wholly personal reflection emanating from a very noble mind, who was an exceptional being for his time and, too, only through suicide escaped his condemnation to death by the imperial power), the fact remains that slavery nonetheless lived on until the period called the High

Middle Ages. The historians of ancient Rome saw no more evil in it than did the Romans themselves, and, as long as exclusive and indiscriminate admiration for classical antiquity lasted, which is to say from the sixteenth century up to our own time, no one could be found to denounce this enormous flaw in a society so commended as an example. Even Bossuet set himself the task of demonstrating that slavery was according to the "natural law". On the other hand, these same historians were indignant about medieval serfdom, so characteristic of those dark centuries where ignorance and tyranny reigned. Even today, moreover, a certain number of academics, in the obvious concern to simplify the question, translate the word *servus* by *slave* in the texts of the twelfth century. In doing so, they are in formal contradiction to the history of law and customs of the time they are dealing with, but they gain in moral comfort. Some use more subtle ways, such as the one who, in speaking of the slavery practiced in the Muslim world, declared that the other residents of the Mediterranean during the Carolingian period *must* also have bought and sold slaves. Is this "must" acceptable on the level of historical rigor? [1]

Let us pass over these fantasies. The fact is, there is no comparison between the ancient *servus*, the slave, and the

[1] All the less acceptable since there is some evidence—extremely rare, it is true—still extant of sales or purchases of slaves in the Muslim Near East, of which some traces are found, for example, in Marseille notary records in the middle of the thirteenth century. Incontestable proof that the southern tradesmen who had connections with barbarian lands did not fail to participate in a commerce expressly forbidden by the Church and condemned by the customs of the times. But it was at that time in the same proportions and under the same conditions as the slave trade that began, still at Marseille, at the end of the nineteenth century, even at the beginning of the twentieth, when it was practiced by several rather unscrupulous shipowners without regard for civil laws and well after the general prohibition of slavery.

medieval *servus*, the serf. Because the one was a thing and the other a man. The meaning of the human person experienced a change between ancient times and medieval times, a slow change, because slavery was deeply rooted in the customs of Roman society in particular, but an irreversible one. And, in consequence, slavery, which is perhaps the most profound temptation of humanity, could thereafter no longer be practiced in complete good conscience.

The substitution of serfdom for slavery is without a doubt the social fact that best emphasizes the disappearance of the influence of Roman law, of Roman mentality, in Western societies from the fifth and sixth centuries on. When Salvianus, the Marseille priest, cried out at the fall of the empire: "The sole wish of the Romans [by which we should understand the peoples submitted to Rome] is never to have to fall again under the yoke of Rome", he expressed a feeling of liberation very close to that experienced by decolonized peoples today. In fact, the two situations are equivalent (acknowledging inevitable differences: What historian would dare maintain that history could repeat itself?). That consciousness of a people freed from Roman imperialism, from its institutions, its functionaries, and its merchants, is that which lives at present in so many peoples of Africa and Asia.

In spite of the very appreciable benefits, which were, moreover, justly appreciated by the victims of Roman colonization, the latter, once the empire had collapsed, accommodated the original customs of the various peoples of the West whose affinities with the "barbarians" were evident. These Celtic and Germanic peoples knew slavery only in a very mitigated form, which was not in contradiction with Christianity: so the medieval serf was indeed a person and treated as such; his master did not have over him the right of life and death that Roman law recognized. Besides, far more than a determined juridical category, serfdom was a state, tied to an essentially rural and land-based mode of life; it obeyed agricultural imperatives and, above all, that necessary stability that a land-based culture implies. In the society we see come into being during the sixth and seventh centuries, life was organized around the soil that nourishes, and the serf was the one of whom stability was demanded: he had to remain on the domain; he was obliged to cultivate, to dig, rake, sow, and also harvest; for if he was forbidden to leave this land, he knew that he would have his part of its harvest. In other words, the lord of the domain could not expel him any more than the serf could "clear out". It was this intimate connection between man and the soil on which he lived that constituted serfdom, for, in all other respects, the serf had all the rights of the free man: he could marry, establish a family, his land, as well as the goods he was able to acquire, would pass to his children after his death. The lord, let us note, had, although obviously on a totally different scale, the same obligations as the serf, for he could neither sell nor give up his land nor desert it.

The situation of the serf, as we see, was radically different and in no way comparable to that of the slave, who did not have the right to marry or establish a family or to avail himself in any way of the dignity of the human person: he was an object that could be bought and sold and over which the power of another man, his master, was unlimited.

In the memory of the people of my generation, the medieval serf evoked, through an association of ideas, a long concert of frogs. According to our school textbooks, in fact, he spent most of his time beating ponds in order to quiet the frogs who prevented the lord from sleeping. That so absurd a fable could find an audience—and it was mentioned in texts from the beginning of the seventeenth century on—

proves a certain revenge of the imaginary over the rational: no one even sought to know which might have made more noise, the frog—even allowing that one could have made it be quiet—or the man occupied with beating the pond. A lot of literature has also been written about this man of the earth, this unassuming, anonymous being, of whom we have no documentary evidence. This picture is only partially true, for an attentive perusal of our archival documents would permit us, in many cases, to reconstitute the very history of the serfs, and that is what a historian like Jacques Boussard has been able to do, with accuracy and skill.[2] A study of the cartulary of the Ronceray abbey allowed him to reconstruct the history of a serf, Constant Le Roux: a man very much our own, from the countless line of Le Grands, Le Forts, Le Roux of all kinds, whose life and activity, as humble as they were, emerge from the study of apparently very insignificant acts, those testimonies, lists, contracts, deeds of donations, exchanges, and so on, whose potential riches are far from having been exhausted.

This Constant Le Roux, serf of the lord of Chantoceaux in Anjou, lived in the last years of the eleventh century. He was a relentless worker, endowed as well with an instinctive cunning that allowed him to miss no occasion to increase his plot of land: the religious of the monastery of Ronceray entrusted him with the custody of a storeroom near the church of Saint-Évroult and some vines in the locality of Doutre. Then it was the countess of Anjou who made him a gift of another storeroom, near the ramparts of Angers. The nuns of Ronceray, who had inherited a house, a bakery, and some vines located quite close to Constant's storeroom, around

[2] J. Boussard, in "La Vie en Anjou du IX^e au XIII^e siècle", Le Moyen âge 56 (1950): 29, 68.

the Chanzé gate, found it practical to put him in charge of
the whole thing as a life income; a little later, they increased
the portion by adding to it the land of Espau, including mead-
ows and pastureland. Soon Constant, who was married, grew
weary of his state as a worker for a half-share of the produce;
by dint of his insistence with the religious, he managed to
get them to agree to lease their lands to him, which was
much more advantageous to him. He increased his enterprise again with a vineyard at Beaumont, some two acres
near Roche-de-Chanzé. Then, not having any children, he
got the nuns to agree that his lands might devolve upon his
nephew Gautier, while his niece Yseut would marry the cel-
lerer of the abbey, Rohot. Finally, his history being to the
end typical of the times, late in life, he entered the abbey of
Saint-Aubin as a monk, while his wife was admitted as a nun
at Ronceray.

Let me add that, for whoever is willing to study the documents, many like Constant Le Roux would come to light,
endowed with the same tenacity and ending in the same humble success. I am thinking, for example, of that deed once
exhibited in the museum of French history in which one
saw two serfs, named Auberede and Romelde, who, at the
end of the eleventh century (between 1089 and 1095), bought
their freedom in exchange for a house they owned in the
marketplace of Beauvais; which is enough to prove that serfs
(in this case female serfs) had at that time the possibility of
owning their own property.

That being stated, it is obvious that the condition of the
serf must not have been very enviable and that freeing serfs
was a pious work. The most ancient cartularies contain multiple acts of emancipation, concerning sometimes one hundred, two hundred, five hundred serfs; sometimes, too, only
a single family, indeed, a single man. It was the same with serf-

dom as it was with all restriction of man's freedom: considered supportable as long as it was a reciprocal arrangement imposed by vital necessities, it became intolerable from the moment when the man could assure his living by himself. The peasant was able to consider it an appreciable benefit to live on a domain from which he could not be expelled; but when he was able to find his living elsewhere than on the domain, if he thought himself better suited for traveling and commerce, he preferred freedom. This is what happened especially at the time of urban expansion, from the end of the tenth century through the eleventh century; those who were gathered together on the land of a new town belonging to a lord asked first and foremost to be able to come and go freely, a faculty refused to serfs and indispensable to tradesmen.

I had occasion to collect the reminiscences of an old farm worker whose age no longer allowed him to travel and who was going to end his days in a poorhouse: "I have worked this land all my life without having a square meter to myself"; compared to that of the medieval serf, his fate would appear infinitely less fortunate: as a serf of the lord on a domain, he would have been assured of ending his life there peacefully; nothing would have belonged to him as his own, but the use of it could not have been withdrawn from him. And, from this point of view, the serf had the same relation to the land as the lord himself: the latter never possessed it in full ownership as we understand it today; ownership belonged to his descendants; he could sell or alienate only the secondary belongings that came to him through personal inheritance, but over the principal domain he had only a right of usage.

This is the specific characteristic of the period, this particular conception of the relations of man and earth, into which the notion of full and complete ownership did not enter. A characteristic of Roman law, ownership, the right to "use and abuse", did not exist in our medieval customs, which knew only usage; and usage, moreover, that was most of the time burdened with multiple easements: the right of the peasant of the place to pasture his animals in the forest of the domain, the right to take wood from it for building or for his fireplace, and so on. All-powerful custom thus ruled a play of interdependences that made an extremely dense fabric of medieval society. Complex for historians, it was no less so for contemporaries; it was necessary to have recourse to the eldest in the land in order to settle disputes and to know in what manner the custom of a particular locality ruled a particular problem. There was in this, too, a radical opposition between ancient society and medieval society, but there is also for us, who are formed by Roman law, an extreme difficulty in understanding how relations between one man and another and between man and the earth were set up in medieval times. The remnants of the laws of usage that, in certain parts of the country, persisted very far into the nineteenth century and, indeed, even into the beginning of the twentieth century, are remembered today only in language (thus the terms *vain pâture* [common grazing land], *défends* [area where access is forbidden to grazing animals]).

The example of Counozouls in Aude, which I cited in my *Histoire de la bourgeoisie*,[3] illustrates perfectly the difference in nature between feudal usage and Roman ownership. In this village, despite the civil code in general, and more particularly the forestry code, which, since 1827, has set the rules for the conditions of forest management, the inhabitants had been able to preserve, even to the beginning of the twentieth century, the rights of usage they possessed from time immemorial over the woods surrounding the district. So, when the new owner

---

[3] *Histoire de la bourgeoisie en France* (Paris: Éd. du Seuil, 1962), 2:588–89.

of these woods, an industrialist named Jodot, who had bought them from La Rochefoucauld,[4] intended to enforce what he could legitimately treat according to the law as his particular property, he ran into fierce opposition from the villagers. Even today, one could say that the inhabitants of Counozouls are living in the Middle Ages—this time without misusing the term! But in order to do that, they had to give proof of a spirit of harmony and of quite uncommon cohesion, to the point of declaring themselves a "free republic" and to sending one of their own to study law at Toulouse in order to be better able to defend themselves and protect the rights of usage over those woods that assure their prosperity.

In the final analysis, in our Western countries, the bond of serfdom acted as a benefit for the peasant. In the countries of Central and Eastern Europe, the free peasant was exposed to all the dangers, all the insecurity that is still suffered by a great number of the peasants of Africa and Asia (to begin with, through that terrible factor of compulsory sale that occurred when a man of the land went into debt to a moneylender, to a usurer who obliged him to sell his harvest uncut; but that is another story!). It was only much later, during the classical period and in modern times, that, through the example set in Slavic lands, a form of serfdom was born that was infinitely harder than that of the Western peasants in the Middle Ages. The latter, in the fourteenth century, as a contributing factor to the weakening of the nobility, had in practical terms the possession of the land they cultivated. But, from the seventeenth century on, particularly in France (from the sixteenth century in England), the way of passing on the

---

[4] Like other ancient lords, the latter had let stand the rights of usage that the peasants had enjoyed over their lands from the earliest times up to the Revolution.

land changed. The appropriation that Jean-Jacques Rousseau observed came, not as he thought, from property orig-
inally held in common that had been fenced (although in
England, for example, the struggle crystallized precisely around
fences), but from the fact that arable land was, from the Ancien Régime on, the object of sale and purchase, which it
was not, except in an extremely restrained measure, during
feudal times. Consequently one sees, especially near towns,
those who had money—shopkeepers, members of parlia-
ment, royal functionaries—buy land, while the share of the
peasant was limited and henceforth poorly protected.

A complete account of the question would require a whole
course in the history of law; without elaborating more about
it, and in order to return to serfdom, let me point out, among
other disadvantages, that in a very hierarchical society like
that of the Middle Ages, the condition of the serf implied an
inferior position, somewhat comparable to that of someone
of mixed race up until a period close to our own. For a free
man, particularly if he was noble, to marry a serf was to de-
mean himself; in a time when the social group was considered to have rights over the individual and vice versa, such a
misalliance was the cause of tensions. Consequently, one
sought hard to free oneself from serfdom, for example through
some amount of money. The Church, herself a source of
social mobility, greatly encouraged the emancipation of serfs.
Let us recall the very striking example of Suger, the son of
serfs, who had nonetheless been the fellow student of the
future King Louis VI at the abbey of Saint-Denis; on their
school benches was born a friendship that must have ceased
only with their lives; and we know that, once he himself had
become the abbot of Saint-Denis, Suger governed the kingdom during the crusade of Louis VII, who, on his return,
proclaimed him "Father of the Country".

Whatever might have been the advantages and the drawbacks, there was a great distance between medieval serfdom and the renaissance of slavery that was abruptly produced in the sixteenth century in the colonies of America. Now, that was a matter of real slavery, of persons considered and treated as things, sold and shipped as cargo of ordinary merchandise. It was this very return to slavery determined by colonial expansion that characterized the classical period. And, as in antiquity, the humanism esteemed during that period does not seem to have brought any attention to that portion of humanity that was enslaved.

Yet it seems unquestionable that the renewed influence of antiquity played a part in justifying this unjustifiable commerce. When, in the first half of the sixteenth century, controversies set the Dominicans like Bartolomé de Las Casas or Vitoria against the lawyers of Salamanca, these latter took as their authority the example of the *Pax Romana* to combat the arguments of the religious that denounced before the king of Spain the iniquity of the wars of conquest and of proslavery politics.[5] Their efforts were not going to stop the peoples of Europe from subjugating those of America, Africa, and then in part of Asia in order to reap economic and political profits from them. With time, the importance of a state would come to be measured by its colonial power. And that at the price of wars that would be more and more difficult, and thanks to the methodical organization of the African slave trade, which brought massive cargoes of slaves to the new continent, for example, for the cultivation of sugar cane in the Antilles. It was the famous "triangular commerce";

[5] See the work by M. Mahn-Lot, *La Découverte de l'Amérique*, Questions d'histoire, no. 18 (Paris: Flammarion, 1970), particularly 83f. It would also be good to read the texts translated and introduced by the same author: *B. de Las Casas: L'Évangile et la force* (Paris: Éd. du Cerf, 1964).

the negotiators, primarily English but also French, Spanish, and Portuguese, coming to buy slaves on the coasts of Africa in order to resell them to the planters of the Antilles, Guyana, and so forth. We should also mention here the wholesale genocides that would be produced, particularly in the nineteenth century, beginning with the methodical annihilation of the Indians of North America. And if at the end of our own twentieth century the apartheid of South Africa seemed an inadmissible anachronism, it would certainly not be without interest to recall that in some countries like Australia and New Zealand, the question of apartheid is no longer even posed: all the natives have been massacred.[6]

To return to France and the classical period, it will suffice to recall Colbert and the Sun King at Versailles, ruling in all good conscience on questions concerning the condition of slaves in the Antilles and creating or encouraging the commercial companies through which their traffic was carried out. The result was the wealth of cites like Bordeaux, Nantes, La Rochelle. To be just, one must add that only France worked out a kind of code tending toward the protection of black slaves—a very Platonic disposition, moreover, when one knows that whites were charged with overseeing its application. This state of things, as we know, lasted in reality up until that first true start of liberation: the 1848 Revolution—that of 1793 having only very temporarily abolished slavery in written texts without any practical effect. We know that, in English-speaking regions, slavery was to persist up to the War of Secession, and later still in Brazil.

---

[6] At the request of the ambassadors of Australia and New Zealand, we will give here the population statistics: Australia, 12.5 million inhabitants, of which 150,000 are aborigines; New Zealand, according to the 1961 census, had 2.5 million, of which 168,000 were aborigines. We will leave to the reader the task of evaluating the statistics.

# 6

# WOMEN WITHOUT SOULS

In 1975, that "year of the woman", the rate of references to the Middle Ages became staggering; the image of the Middle Ages, of the dark, obscure times from which we emerged, like Truth from the well, was thrust upon all minds and furnished a fundamental theme for treatises, colloquia, symposia, and seminars of all kinds. When I mentioned one day in public the name of Eleanor of Aquitaine, I immediately received enthusiastic approval: "What an admirable person!" one of the people present exclaimed. "In a time when women thought only of having children . . ." I pointed out to her that Eleanor seemed to have thought about it also, since she had ten of them and since, given her personality, that could not have happened through mere inadvertence. The enthusiasm cooled a bit.

The status of women in France in the Middle Ages is today [1977] a nearly new subject; few serious studies have been devoted to it, no more, one might say, than could be counted on the fingers of one hand. The Jean Bodin Society, whose works are so remarkable, published between 1959 and 1962 two large volumes (346 and 770 pages respectively) on *La Femme*. All civilizations are examined successively. Women in the Society of Siam, or according to the various cuneiform laws, or in the Malikite-Maghreb law, are masterfully studied in it, but, for our medieval West, we find only ten pages dealing with canon law, ten others dealing with the period running from the thirteenth to the end of the seventeenth century, a study devoted to classical times up to the civil code, another to the French monarchy, and more detailed works on Italy, Belgium, and England in the Middle Ages. That is absolutely all. The feudal period is passed over in complete silence.

It is equally useless to look there for a study on women in the Celtic societies, where nevertheless we are certain they held a role quite in contrast to the one in which they were restricted in societies of the classical Greco-Roman type. In what concerns the Celts, for the historians of our time, men and women were on a strictly equal footing, since neither one nor the other is ever mentioned. The Celts are, once and for all, refused any right of existence.

And yet, one image commands attention that I have had occasion to mention elsewhere.[1] Is it not surprising, in fact, to think that in feudal times the queen was crowned just like the king, generally in Reims, sometimes in other cathedrals of the royal domain (at Sens for Margaret of Provence), but always by the hands of the archbishop of Reims? In other words, as much importance was attributed to the crowning of the queen as to that of the king. Now, the last queen who was crowned was Marie de Médicis; this was done belatedly, in 1610, on the very eve of the death of her spouse, Henry IV. The ceremony took place in Paris according to a custom that had arisen in the preceding centuries (getting to Reims at that time represented a military action because of the Anglo-French wars). And besides, from these medieval times (the term taken here in contrast to feudal times), the crowning of

---

[1] *Histoire de la bourgeoisie en France* (Paris: Éd. du Seuil, 1962), 2:30–31.

the queen had assumed less importance than that of the king; in a period when war reigned in France as an endemic state (that of the famous Hundred Years' War), military needs began to prevail over any other preoccupation, and the king was first of all a war chief. Still, it was only in the seventeenth century that the queen literally disappeared from the scene in favor of the "favorite". It is enough to recall the destiny of Marie-Thérèse or that of Marie Leszcynska to be convinced of that. And when the last queen wanted to reassume a particle of power, she was given the occasion to repent of it, since she was named Marie Antoinette (it is only fair to add that the last favorite, Du Barry, joined the last queen on the scaffold).

This rapid skimming through the status of queens gives an accurate enough idea of what happened for women in general; the place they held in society, the influence they exercised, followed an exactly parallel line. While women like Eleanor of Aquitaine and Blanche of Castile really dominated their century, while they unquestionably exercised power when the king was absent, sick, or dead, while they had their chancellery, their dower, their field of personal activity (which could be claimed as a fruitful example by the most feminist movements of our time), the woman in classical times was relegated to the background; she exercised power only in a hidden way and found herself excluded from any political or administrative function. She was even considered, especially in Latin countries, as being incapable of ruling, of succeeding to a fiefdom or domain, and, finally, according to our Code, of exercising any right whatsoever over her personal property.

It is as always in the history of law that we must seek the facts and their meaning, in other words, the reason for this decline, which became, in the nineteenth century, the total disappearance of the role of woman, especially in France. Her influence diminished in direct proportion to the rise of Roman law in juridical studies, then in institutions, and finally in customs. It was a progressive obliteration, whose principal stages, in France at least, one can follow very easily.

Curiously enough, the first provision that excluded women from the succession to the throne was made by Philip the Fair. The fact is that this king was under the influence of the southern French jurists, who had literally invaded the court of France at the beginning of the fourteenth century and who, as typical representatives of the urban bourgeoisie, particularly of cities of the south, who were much into trading, rediscovered Roman law with a veritable intellectual avidity. This law, which had been conceived for the military, functionaries, and merchants, conferred on the property owner the *jus utendi et abutendi*, the right of use and abuse, in complete contradiction to the customary law of that time but eminently favorable to those who held personal wealth. To the latter, this legislation seemed, and rightly so, infinitely superior to the existing customs for insuring and protecting goods, trade, and commerce. Roman law, whose influence is seen reborn in Italy, particularly in Bologne, was the great temptation of the medieval period; it was studied with enthusiasm not only by the urban bourgeoisie but also by all those who saw in it an instrument of centralization and authority. It showed in large part the effects of its imperialist and, let us say the word, colonialist origins. It was the law par excellence of those who wanted to affirm a central state authority. So it was claimed, adopted, extended by the powers seeking centralization at that time: by the emperor, first of all, then by the papacy. In the middle of the thirteenth century, Emperor Frederick II, whose tendencies were those of a monarch, made it the common law of the German countries. The university he founded in Naples—the only one the subjects of the emperor would henceforth be authorized to attend—dispensed the study of Roman law, so well, in fact, that it was this Roman law that ruled the institutions and customs of the Germanic countries at a time when the West did not yet allow it.[2] It would only be in the course of the seventeenth century that the study of Roman law, precisely because it was imperial law, would be allowed at the University of Paris. The fact is that, much earlier, it was taught at Toulouse and that, favored by the infatuation felt in the sixteenth century for antiquity, it had begun to penetrate the customs and to modify profoundly the habits and mentalities in France itself.

Now Roman law is no more favorable to the woman than it is to the child. It is a monarchical law, which allows only one single end. It is the law of the *pater familias*, father, proprietor, and, in his own home, high priest, the head of the family with sacred, in any case unlimited, power in what concerns his children: he has the right of life and death over them—it is the same for his wife, despite some limitations belatedly introduced during the Byzantine Empire.

It was by relying on Roman law that jurists like Dumoulin, through their treatises and their teaching, contributed both to extending the power of the centralized state and also—what interests us here—to restricting the freedom of women and their capacity for action, particularly in marriage. The influence of this law would be so strong that in the sixteenth century the age of majority, which for the most part was twelve years for girls and fourteen for boys, was returned to

[2] Paradoxically, the Germanic countries were thus formed by Roman law, while in France, with all due respect to those who remain attached to the myth of the "Latin race", the customs were formed by usages believed to be "Germanic" but which should have been called, rather, "Celtic".

the very age fixed in Rome, that is, twenty-five years (in Rome majority scarcely mattered, since the power of the father over his children remained effective all during his life). This was a clear regression from what had been customary, which permitted a child to acquire true autonomy when very young, without, for all that, withdrawing him from the solidarity of the family. Within this latter structure, the father had a managerial, not proprietary, authority: he did not have the power to disinherit his oldest son. This was the custom that also regulated the transmission of property in noble or common families, in a sense that shows very well, moreover, the power the woman maintained over what belonged to her as her own: in the case of a deceased couple without any direct heir, the property originating from the father went to the paternal family, but that originating from the mother returned to the maternal family, according to the well-known adage of common law: *paterna paternis, materna maternis.*

In the seventeenth century, already, we note a profound evolution of this point of view: children, considered as minors until twenty-five years old, remained under paternal power, and the character of ownership as the monopoly of the father became only more pronounced. The Napoleonic Code put the final touch to this system and gave an imperative sense to tendencies that had begun to assert themselves from the end of the medieval period. Let us recall that it was only in the twelfth century that women were obliged to take the name of their spouse; and also that it was only with the Council of Trent, thus in the second half of the sixteenth century, that the consent of parents became necessary for the marriage of children; just as the sanction of the Church became indispensable. To the old adage of former times:

Drink, eat, sleep together
Get married, I think

is added:

but the Church must get involved in it.

Here I must remark on the number of unions duly arranged by families during feudal times: girls and boys engaged from the cradle, promised to each other; examples in fact abound. This is without fail used as the argument when demonstrating that women were not free during the period; to which it is easy to retort that, from this point of view, boys and girls found themselves on rigorously equal footing, for the future groom was disposed of in absolutely the same way as the future bride. Yet, it is incontestable that there occurred at that time what still happens today in two-thirds of the world: the great majority of unions were arranged by families. And in noble, even royal families, these dispositions constituted in a way part of the duties of birth, for a marriage between two heirs of fiefdoms or kingdoms was considered the best way to seal a peace treaty, to assure reciprocal friendliness, and also to provide a fruitful legacy for the future.

One power fought against these imposed unions, and that was the Church; she increased the number of the causes of nullity in canon law, never ceased to claim freedom for those who were pledged to each other, and often proved rather indulgent in tolerating in fact the rupture of imposed bonds—much more at that time, we should note, than later. It is, moreover, an established fact, taken from simple evidence, that everywhere progress in free choice of a spouse accompanied progress in the spread of Christianity. Even today, it is in Christian lands that this freedom, so justly demanded, is

recognized by law, while in Muslim lands or in the countries
of the Far East this freedom, which seems essential to us,
does not exist or has only very recently been granted.[3]

That leads us to discuss the expression "a Church hostile
to women". We will not pause here to take up the whole of
a question that would necessitate a volume by itself; neither
will we go on to discuss the obvious nonsense that has been
uttered in this regard. "It was only in the fifteenth century
that the Church admitted that women had a soul." This statement was candidly affirmed one day on the radio by some
writer of fiction who was no doubt motivated by good in-
tentions but whose information showed proof of several la-
cunae! So, for centuries, soul-less beings were baptized,
confessed, and admitted to the Eucharist! How strange that
the first martyrs honored as saints were women and not men:
Saint Agnes, Saint Cecilia, Saint Agatha, and so many others. How truly sad that Saint Blandine and Saint Genevieve
were deprived of immortal souls. How surprising that one
of the most ancient catacomb paintings (in the burial ground
of Priscilla) represented precisely the *Virgin with Child*, well
designated by the star and the prophet Isaiah. And finally,
whom shall we believe, those who, justly, reproach the medieval Church for the cult of the Virgin Mary or those who
judge the Virgin to have been considered at that time to be
a creature without a soul?

Without letting such nonsense delay us, we will merely
recall here that some women (who were not in any particular way singled out by their family or their birth, since they

---

[3] "Muslim legislation forbids the woman what she demands today and what
she calls her rights and what constitutes nothing but aggression against the
rights that have been conferred on men alone." So Sheik Hasanam Makhluf
expressed himself in 1952, in the publication entitled *Al Misri* (see *La Documentation française*, no. 2418 [May 31, 1952], 4).

came, as we would say today, from all social strata, as witnessed by the shepherdess of Nanterre) enjoyed in the Church, and by their function in the Church, an extraordinary power during the Middle Ages. Certain abbesses were feudal lords whose power was respected equally with that of other lords; some wore the cross just like a bishop; they often administered vast territories with villages, parishes . . . One example among thousands of others: in the middle of the twelfth century, the cartularies permit us to follow the formation of the monastery of the Paraclete whose superior was Héloïse; one need only skim through them to note that the life of an abbess of that period included a whole administrative aspect: donations were accumulated that allowed, here, the collection of a tithe on a vineyard, there, the right to rent on hay or corn, here to have a barn, and there a right of pasture in the forest . . . Her activity was also that of an owner, indeed, of a lord. This is to say that, by their religious functions, certain women exercised, even in secular life, a power that many men would envy today.

On the other hand, one notes that the religious of that time—about whom, we should say in passing, serious research is completely lacking—were for the most part extremely well-educated women who could have rivaled the most learned monks of the time in their knowledge. Héloïse herself knew and taught Greek and Hebrew to her nuns. It was from an abbey of women, that of Gandersheim, that a manuscript came in the tenth century containing six comedies in rhymed prose in imitation of Terence; they have been attributed to the famous abbess Hroswitha, whose influence, moreover, on the literary development of the Germanic lands is well known. These comedies, probably enacted by the religious, are, from the point of view of dramatic history, considered to be proof of a scholarly tradition that contributed to the development of theatre in the Middle Ages. Let us add in passing that many of the monasteries of men and women dispensed local instruction to children of the region.

It is surprising, also, to note that the best-known encyclopedia of the twelfth century came from a woman religious, the abbess Herrad of Landsberg. It was the famous *Hortus deliciarum, Garden of Delights*, in which scholars draw the most reliable information about the state of technical knowledge of that time. Just as much could be said for the works of the famous Hildegarde of Bingen. Finally, another woman religious, Gertrude of Helfta, in the thirteenth century, tells us how happy she was to pass from the state of "grammarian" to that of "theologian", which is to say that, after having gone through the stage of preparatory studies, she reached the higher stage, like that studied at the University. Which proves that in the thirteenth century, convents of women were still what they had always been since the time of Saint Jerome, who established the first of them, the community of Bethlehem: centers of prayer, but also of religious knowledge, exegesis, learning; Sacred Scripture was studied there, considered as the basis of all knowledge, and also all the elements of religious and secular learning. The religious were educated girls; moreover, entering a convent was a normal path for those who wanted to develop their knowledge beyond the usual level. What seemed extraordinary in Héloïse in her youth was the fact that, not being a religious and not manifesting any desire to enter a convent, she nevertheless pursued very dry studies instead of contenting herself with the more frivolous, more carefree life of a girl wanting to "remain in the world". The letter that Peter the Venerable sent to her explicitly says so.

But there are more surprising things yet. If one wants to get an exact idea of the place held by women in the Church in feudal times, one must wonder what would be said in our twentieth century of convents of men placed under the authority of a woman. Would a project of this kind have the least chance of succeeding in our time? This was, however, achieved with great success and without providing the least scandal in the Church by Robert d'Arbrissel at Fontevrault, in the early part of the twelfth century. Having resolved to situate the extraordinary crowd of men and woman who were following in his footsteps—for he was one of the great converters of all time—Robert d'Arbrissel decided to found two convents, one for men and the other for women;[4] between them rose the church, which was the only place where the monks and nuns could meet. Now this double monastery was placed under the authority, not of an abbot, but of an abbess. The latter, through the will of the founder, was to be a widow, having had the experience of marriage. Let us add, to complete the picture, that the first abbess, Petronilla of Chemillé, who presided over the fortunes of this order of Fontevrault, was twenty-two years old. Such audacity would not have the least chance of being envisaged again in our own time.

If one examines the facts, the conclusion is inescapable: during the whole feudal period, the place of women in the Church was certainly different from that of men (and is this not precisely a proof of the wisdom of making allowances for what equal but different creatures men and women are?), but it was an eminent place, which, moreover, symbolized perfectly the cult, which was likewise eminent, rendered to the Virgin among all the saints. And it is scarcely surprising that the period ends with a woman's face: that of Joan of Arc,

---

[4] There were numerous other double orders during the period, notably in Anglo-Saxon regions and in Spain.

who, let us say in passing, could never have obtained in later centuries the audience or aroused the confidence that she obtained in the end.

It is surprising, too, to observe the growing intransigence that occurred with respect to women at the very end of the thirteenth century. It was through a very significant measure that Pope Boniface VIII, in 1298, decided on the total and strict cloister of nuns (Carthusians and Cistercians) that they have known ever since. In consequence, women religious would no longer be allowed to mix with the world. Consecrated laywomen, such as the béguines, who, in the thirteenth century, led a life like everyone else's but were consecrated by vows, would no longer be tolerated. In the seventeenth century, in particular, the Visitation sisters, meant by their foundress to mix in everyday life, were obliged to adapt themselves to the same cloister as the Carmelites; so that Saint Vincent de Paul, in order to permit the Daughters of Charity to render service to the poor, to go care for the sick and to help families in need, was very careful not to treat them as religious and make them take the veil; if he had, their fate would have been that of the Visitandines. It was by then inconceivable for a woman, having decided to consecrate her life to God, not to be cloistered; although in the new orders created for men, such as the Jesuits, the latter remained in the world.

It suffices to say that the status of women in the Church is exactly the same as their status in civil society and that gradually, after the Middle Ages, everything that conferred on them any autonomy, any independence, any instruction, was taken away from them. Now, at the very time when the University—which admitted only men—was trying to concentrate knowledge and teaching, convents gradually ceased to be those centers of study that they had been previously;

let us add that they also ceased, and rather rapidly, being centers of prayer. Women thus found themselves excluded from ecclesial life just as from intellectual life. The movement was precipitated when, at the beginning of the sixteenth century, the king of France had control over the nomination of abbesses and abbots. The best example remains the order of Fontevrault, which became a sanctuary for old mistresses of the king. A sanctuary where, moreover, a less and less edifying life was led, for such strict cloister was not long in suffering violence, acknowledged or not. If some orders, like those of Carmel or the Poor Clares, kept their purity thanks to reforms, most of the monasteries of women, at the end of the Ancien Régime, were accessible houses where the younger daughters of large families received a large number of visits and where cards were played, as well as other "forbidden games", very far into the night.

We have yet to speak of women who were neither great ladies nor abbesses nor even nuns: peasants and townswomen, mothers of families and women practicing a trade. It goes without saying that, to be treated correctly, such questions would demand several volumes and would also require preliminary works that have not been written. It would be indispensable to explore not only collections of customs and town statutes but also the enormous mass of notarial acts, in the south especially, cartularies, legal documents, or even the inquiries ordered by Saint Louis;[5] we find there, taken from

---

[5] An unprecedented and, moreover, short-lived initiative, which consisted in the king's having made a survey of his own administration by directly addressing those administered: the king sent out on-site investigators uniquely charged to gather together the responses of common folk who had made complaints to royal agents and to reverse thus, on site, the abuse committed; in other words, this was the efficacious way to remedy the failures of state control.

everyday life, thousands of small details, gleaned by chance and without any preconceived order, which show us men and women through the small facts of existence: here the complaint of a woman hairdresser, there of a woman salt merchant (trading in salt), of a woman miller, of the widow of a farmer, of a chatelaine, of a woman Crusader, and so on.

It is through documents of this kind that one can, piece by piece, reconstruct, as in a mosaic, the real story. There is no point in saying that this story is in appearance something very different from that provided by the *chansons de geste*, the chivalric novels, and the literary sources that have so often been taken as historical sources!

The picture that comes into focus from the whole of these documents presents for us more than one surprising trait, since one sees, for example, women voting like men in urban assemblies or those of rural parishes. I am often amused, in various conferences or reports, to cite the case of Gaillardine de Fréchou, who, at the time of an agreement proposed by the abbey of Saint-Savin to the inhabitants of Cauterets in the Pyrenees, was the only one to vote No, while all the rest of the population voted Yes. The vote of women was not expressly mentioned everywhere, but that may be because the necessity for doing so was not obvious. When texts allow us to differentiate the origin of the votes, we see that, in regions as different as the Béarn parishes, certain villages of Champagne, and certain eastern cities like Pont-à-Mousson, or even in Touraine at the time of the Estate-General of 1308, women are explicitly named among the voters, without anything being said to imply it was a usage particular to the locality. In city statutes, there is a general indication that the votes were received in an assembly of the inhabitants without any further details; sometimes mention is made of age by indicating, as at Aurillac, that the right to vote was exercised at the age of twenty years or, at Embrun, beginning at fourteen years. Let us add that, since generally the votes were cast by home, that is, by household, rather than by individual, it was the one who represented the "home", thus the father, who was called to represent his family; if it was the father of the family who was naturally the head of it, it remained well understood that his authority was that of a manager and an administrator, not an owner.

In notarial acts, it is very common to see a married woman act by herself, in opening, for example, a shop or a trade, and she did so without being obliged to produce her husband's authorization. Finally, the tax rolls (we would say the preceptor's registers), when they have been preserved for us, as in the case of Paris at the end of the thirteenth century, show a host of women plying trades: schoolmistress, doctor, apothecary, plasterer, dyer, copyist, miniaturist, binder, and so on.

It was only at the end of the sixteenth century, through a parliamentary decree dated 1593, that women would be explicitly excluded from all state functions. The growing influence of Roman law was not long, then, in restricting women to what has been, in all times, her privileged domain: the care of the home and education of children—at least up to the moment when that, too, would be taken away by law, for, let us note, with the Napoleonic Code, she would not even be mistress of her own property any more and would play only a subordinate role in her own household. For, from the time of Montaigne up to Jean-Jacques Rousseau, it was men who composed educational treatises, even though the first treatise on education published in France that has come down to us was produced by a woman, Dhuoda, who wrote it (in Latin verse) sometime around 841–843 for the use of her son.[6]

[6] P. Riché, *Dhuoda: Manuel pour mon fils* (Paris: Éd. du Cerf, 1975).

Several years ago, some of the discussions that took place on the subject of parental authority in France were rather disconcerting for a historian of the Middle Ages; in fact, the idea that a law was necessary to give women the right to oversee the education of her children would have seemed paradoxical in feudal times. At that time, the married community, both father and mother, exercised jointly the task of educating and protecting children as well as, eventually, administering their property. It is true that the family was conceived then in a much broader sense; education posed infinitely fewer problems, because it was carried out within the heart of a vital fabric, of a familial community that was more extensive and more diversified than in our time, since it was not restricted to the initial mother-father-child cell but included also grandparents, other relatives, and domestics, in the etymological sense of the word. Which did not prevent the child from having, eventually, a distinct legal status; thus, if he inherited his own property (bequeathed by an uncle, for example), this was administered by the family community, which, subsequently, would have to render him an account of it.

There is no shortage of detailed examples furnished by the history of law and customs attesting to the erosion of the place held by women between the time of feudal customs and the triumph of a "Roman" legislation with which our legal code is still permeated. At that time, moreover, when moralists wanted to see "the woman of the hearth", it would have been more appropriate to reverse the proposition and insist that the hearth belonged to the woman.

A reaction to this is coming only in our own time. We should add, moreover, that it is very disappointing: everything is happening as if women, overcome with satisfaction at the idea of having penetrated the masculine world, have remained incapable of the additional imagination required to bring to this world her own mark, which is precisely what is lacking in our society. It is enough for her to imitate men, to be judged capable of practicing the same trades, of adopting the behavior and even the customary clothing of her partner, without even asking herself what might be questionable and should be questioned about this. Without asking herself if she might not be motivated by an unconscious, perhaps excessive, admiration of a masculine world she believes it is necessary and sufficient to copy with as much exactitude as possible, even at the loss of her own identity, by denying in advance what is original in her.

Such observations lead us rather far from the feudal world; they can in any case lead us to wish that this feudal world might be a bit better known by those who believe in good faith that women have "finally left the Middle Ages": in point of fact, women have much to do to recover the place that was theirs in the time of Queen Eleanor and Queen Blanche . . .

7

# THE ACCUSING FINGER

When I was preparing a report for the National Archives on the century of Saint Louis, I had handed to a quite well-educated assistant the well-known passage from the *Trésor* of Brunetto Latini explaining to his readers, in the midst of the thirteenth century, that the earth was round. "What!" she said to me, very astonished, "I thought that Galileo had been burned alive in the Middle Ages for having said that the earth was round."

I explained to her that her comment contained three historical errors: Galileo did not discover that the earth was round; this had been known for more than four centuries. Next, he had not been burned alive, but only imprisoned, which was quite in itself a very discourteous way of treating someone who noticed for the first time that the earth turned around the sun. Finally, the whole thing did not take place in the Middle Ages. But to convince her, I had to have recourse to the twenty-volume Larousse. It was with intense astonishment that she had to admit that the "Galileo affair", which everyone freely attributes to the Middle Ages, belongs very much to the classical period, since it took place in 1633. Galileo, born in 1564, dead in 1642, was a contemporary of Descartes; he was his elder by thirty-two years but died only eight years before he did. The Galileo affair took

115

place one hundred years after the birth of Montaigne (1533), more than a hundred years after the Reformation (1520), nearly two hundred years after the invention of the printing press, and, finally, more than half a century after the Council of Trent (1547–1563), which can justly be regarded as the demarcation between the medieval Church and the Church of classical times.

Let us add, moreover, that the Galileo affair is typical of the classical mentality if one takes the point of view of exegesis.[1]

In the seventeenth century, commentators had a tendency to stick to the literal sense alone; a little like certain exegetes today who are attentive only to the historical sense and reducing Scripture to some empirical data, without admitting, as in the time of Bernard of Clairvaux, that one and the same text might have several levels of meaning, all equally important for the believer.

The Galileo affair was an insult to good sense as well as to the scientific mind. But it is too easily made an insult to history, in that it is not attributed to the period in which it actually evolved, which is to say, to the first half of the seventeenth century.

Now, it is one of the advantages of history that, solely on the strength of dates, we can confront generalizations, theories, and laws. Dates are figures and, thus, a kind of language that, in our age of confusion with languages, remains accessible to all, to the most simple beings just as to the brains

---

[1] In "medieval" times, the methods of explicating texts implied the possibility of commenting on the Bible in ways other than by the literal meaning alone. We are familiar, particularly from the works of Fr. Henri de Lubac (*Exégèse médiévale* [Paris: Aubier, 1959–1962], 4 vols.), with reading "according to the four senses", which accustomed minds to several orders of commentary with respect to the same text: the historical sense, but also the allegorical and moral, and so forth.

most marked by the various sorts of ideological, political, philosophical, even socio-cultural deformations. It is thus with all confidence that one can say that the date of Galileo's condemnation is itself as irrefutable as that of the first step on the moon, as stable as a mathematical law, as fully guaranteed as those planetary revolutions discovered precisely by Galileo. The Galileo trial was contemporary, let us note in passing, with the great age (if one can call it that!) of witchcraft trials. It is known, or rather it is poorly known, that, if there have always been witches and sorcerers, and even more stories of witches and sorcerers, the first trials explicitly mentioned in texts took place only in the fourteenth century in the Toulouse region; after that, we know of the famous one, in 1440, of Gilles de Rais (accused of magic rather than of sorcery, properly speaking). In the second half of the fifteenth century, these trials became more customary, beginning with the one, in 1456 in the Lorraine region, that was to claim eight victims. The interest in witchcraft grew noticeably in the sixteenth century, when serious personages, like Jean Bodin, lawyer and prosecutor for the king, wrote a *Démonomanie* and Nicolas Rémy, judge and general prosecutor for Lorraine, wrote a *Démonolâtrie*; the latter joined, one might say, the practice to the theory, since he sent to the stake, as far as we can judge, some three thousand witches and sorcerers; in fact, with the seventeenth century—the age of reason—the number of witchcraft trials swelled to insane proportions. There was scarcely a region that cannot call to mind famous trials, whether Loudun, Louviers, Nancy, the Méautis affair in Normandy, and so on.[2]

---

[2] On this subject, refer to the summary that appeared in the series entitled Que sais-je? from the Presses universitaires: Jean Palou, *La Sorcellerie*, no. 756, 5th ed. (1975), especially p. 72.

In addition, the most celebrated witchcraft cases occurred in the court itself, that of Louis XIV. No region of Europe was spared, Protestant (England, where the first execution took place under the reign of Elizabeth I in the sixteenth century, Germany, even Sweden and North America) as well as Catholic. The reaction took shape only in the first half of the seventeenth century, with the works of some Jesuits, in particular Fr. Friedrich Spee, whose work *Cautio criminalis,* which appeared in 1633 (the year of the Galileo trial), was not without influence on the judges of his region (Mainz and Würzburg). Pope Urban VIII, in his turn, in 1637, recommended prudence in pursuit of witches and sorcerers. Nevertheless, yet again, in Bordeaux, in 1718, the last of the known witchcraft trials took place, which ended, like its predecessors, at the stake. This should give some cause for reflection to those who have the tendency, without much thought, to join the adjective medieval to the term obscurantism.

To these excesses of superstition it is enough, in fact, to contrast the mentality of feudal times, as expressed, for example, by John of Salisbury, bishop of Chartres in the twelfth century, who said: "The best remedy against this sickness [witchcraft was indeed the subject, and the use of this term by a great thinker brings him curiously close to psychiatrists of today] is to cling firmly to the faith, refuse to listen to those lies, and never to give one's attention to such pitiable follies."

\* \* \*

Respect for religious convictions constitutes today part of the rights of the human person, in the Western world, in any case. It is inscribed in the various declarations of the rights of man. This is undoubtedly one of the points on which progress is evident in the relatively recent past; let us think in particular of the pursuit of Protestants ordered by Louis XIV— or, on the other hand, of the various forms of oppression practiced in Ireland by the English colonists against the Irish Catholics or even in England against the English Catholics, who were subjected to various harassments: we know, for example, that entrance into universities was forbidden them up until 1850.

If we place ourselves back in the mentality of the feudal times, we note that the link between the profane and the sacred was so close that doctrinal deviations took on extreme importance even in everyday life. To take an example often cited, the fact that the Cathars denied the validity of oaths attacked the very essence of feudal life, made up of contracts between one man and another based precisely on the value of the oath. Whence the general reprobation incurred at that time by heresy; it broke a profound accord to which the whole of society adhered, and this rupture seemed to be of extreme gravity to those who witnessed it. Any incident of a spiritual order seemed in this context more serious than a physical casualty.

An actual anecdote is significant from this point of view. Joinville recounts how, at the time when the army of the king of France, of which he was a part, was being ravaged by an epidemic on the banks of the Nile, he himself, recovering from the illness, attended Mass one day from his bed, in his tent. Now, the priest who was celebrating also suddenly suffered an attack of the plague; he faltered. Joinville leapt from his bed and ran to hold him up: "Finish your sacrament", he said; then, continuing his account: "And he finished singing his Mass entirely, and never sang it again." Now, for anyone today, Joinville's action would seem to make little sense: faced with a priest taken ill, one would hurry off to seek a doctor, while Joinville's major preoccupation and that of the priest himself, as far as we can deduce it from the account, was to "finish the sacrament".

Now from many accounts, the Inquisition was the defensive reaction of a society for which, rightly or wrongly, the preservation of the faith seemed as important as physical health is in our day. Here we can put our finger on the differences between one period and another, which is to say, differences of criteria, scale, and value. And it is elementary in history to begin by taking them into account, indeed, by respecting them; otherwise the historian is transformed into a judge.

Nevertheless the institution of the Inquisition is for us the most shocking feature in the whole history of the Middle Ages.[3] A study of it would necessitate an entire library. This library exists, moreover, since the subject has aroused a large number of works, the content of which, however, has not really been made public.[4]

The term "inquisition" means "inquiry"; in the twelfth century, Abelard proclaimed that the life of the searcher, the logician, was spent in "permanent inquisition", and his statement contained nothing that might smack of heresy or call forth repression. The word began to take on a juridical sense

---

[3] So, in some textbooks, one passes directly from the forced baptisms imposed by Charlemagne at the time of the conquest of Saxony to the institution of the Inquisition. That between these two events a half-millennium (450 years at least) elapsed does not in any way trouble the writers: since the Middle Ages definitively form a uniform block in their eyes, they do not see why they should bother.

[4] Let us refer, just once, to the most recent works on a question that has in large part been renewed in recent years, in the present case the *Cahiers de Fanjeaux*, especially devoted to the study of religious history in the southern regions in the Middle Ages, drawn directly from the sources. See particularly numbers 3, *Cathares en Languedoc*; 6, *Le Credo, la Morale et l'Inquisition*; 8, *Les Mendiants en pays d'oc au XIII<sup>e</sup> siècle* (Toulouse: Privat, 1966–1975; the necessary bibliography will be found there).

when, in 1184, Pope Lucius II, at Verona, exhorted bishops to seek out heretics actively in order to evaluate the progression of evil in their diocese. But this was only a definite recommendation to exercise a right the bishop had always had, that of excommunicating heretics; indeed, to "exterminate" them (to banish them, to chase them *ex-terminis*, outside the borders); heretics were multiplying rapidly at the time, especially in the south of France and in Italy. The most numerous, as we know, were those who called themselves by the name of *catharoi*, the pure; the Cathar doctrine can be summed up by saying that it rested on an absolute dualism: the material universe was the work of an evil god, only souls were created by a good god; from which it followed that all that tends toward procreation was to be condemned, marriage in particular; the most pure followers of the doctrine saw in suicide the supreme perfection.[5] In reality, like all sects—and those of our period allow us to understand the phenomenon—this one was very quickly diversified. In the form that spread into Lombardy and in the Provencal and Languedocian regions, Catharism was a religion on two levels: there were the "perfect", who observed the doctrine in all its rigor: absolute continence, the refusal to make war or swear oaths, severe abstinence; while the others, the simple believers, conducted themselves pretty much as they wished; the condition of their salvation depended on absolution, *consolamentum*, which they had to receive from one of the "perfect" ones before their death.

---

[5] If most of the doctrinal writings of the Cathars were destroyed by the tribunals of the Inquisition in the thirteenth century, the most important among them to survive is a polemical treatise coming from one Cathar writing against other Cathars. This was the *Liber de duobus principiis*, by a disciple of the Cathar Jean de Lugio, a dissident of the sect of Desenzano in Italy, which had great importance in the thirteenth century.

As strange as it may seem, it was the Count of Toulouse, Raymond V himself, who was the first to think of fighting with military force the heretics who were swarming over his domain. In a letter to the abbot of Cîteaux, he gives the bleakest description of the extent of the heresy:

> The putrid scourge of heresy has spread to such a point that most of those who consent to it believe they are thereby giving homage to God ... the very ones who have given themselves to the priesthood are corrupted by the plague of heresy, and the holy and ever-venerable premises of the churches remain unkempt; they fall into ruin; baptism is denied; the Eucharist is abominated; penance is scorned; the creation of man and the resurrection of the body are rejected, and all the sacraments of the Church are annulled. As painful as it may be to say, they have gone so far as to introduce two principles [dualism].

In fact, like all heresies, that of the Cathars denied the Incarnation, but it pushed this negation to the point of professing horrible things about the Cross.

Now, when Raymond VI succeeded his father, Raymond V of Toulouse, he had a different attitude toward the heretics; there were even many among his subjects who accused him of favoring them. When in 1208 the pope sent a legate to him, Pierre de Castelnau, Raymond sent him back with threats that aroused a response, for the legate was assassinated two days later. It was at that time that Pope Innocent III began to preach the crusade exhorting the barons of France and elsewhere to take up arms against both the Count of Toulouse and the other heretics of the south.

War was declared, but contrary to what has often been said and written up to now, whether they were the perfect or the simple believers, the heretics were in no way living in hiding. It was in broad daylight that they circulated, preached, and held increasing numbers of discussions and meetings with those who were trying to lead them to orthodoxy, in particular with those mendicant brothers whom Domingo de Guzmán called to the preaching of holy doctrine and to the practice of an integral poverty and who would become in 1215 the Dominicans. The gatherings to which he invited the heretics, the public discussions like those that took place at Fanjeaux—right in the heart of the Albigensian south—and which have remained famous, attest to the fact that, in spite of the episcopal inquiries that had been ordered here and there, the heretics in no way felt the need to hide themselves, and particularly not in those Languedocian regions where they enjoyed an efficacious protection by the southern lords. Everything changed, of course, when war was decided; the change would be even more perceptible when, twenty years later, in 1231, the pontifical Inquisition was instituted.

It was to Pope Gregory IX that the initiative fell, and not to Saint Dominic, as has been absurdly claimed;[6] the latter had been dead ten years when Gregory IX provided for the institution of an ecclesiastical tribunal destined especially for searching out and judging heretics.

The connection between the Dominicans and the Inquisition derives from the fact that this same Gregory IX, when he instituted the Inquisition in 1231, confided responsibility

[6] To be more specific, Saint Dominic had left the Languedocian south by the year 1216 in order to give all his attention to the organization of a religious order whose success surpassed all the hopes of its founder and which would know an astonishing missionary expansion; as early as 1249, the Friars Preachers (they were to be called Dominicans, after the name of their founder) were evangelizing Finland.

for it to the very popular Order of Friars Preachers; but from 1233 on, he added the other principal mendicant order, that of the Friars Minor. The Franciscans exercised inquisitorial functions particularly in Italy, and some also in France, like Étienne de Saint-Thibéry, who, along with his colleague the Dominican Guillaume Arnaud, was massacred in 1242 in Avignonnet.

In spite of what is generally believed, the southerners were not the only ones to be overwhelmed by the Inquisition in the thirteenth century. In fact, the most dramatic actions, those that had the most victims, took place in Burgundy and Champagne as well as in the north of France, falling prey to the redoubtable activities of the notorious Robert le Bougre. The latter was a former heretic who had converted, which accounts for his surname[7] (his true name was Robert le Petit). Having entered the Order of Friars Preachers after his conversion, he was promoted to the duties of inquisitor in 1233 and immediately, at Charité-sur-Loire, ordered executions that aroused the protests of several archbishops, and not minor ones, since among them were the bishops of Reims, Sens, and Bourges. The pope suspended his powers in 1234 but returned them to him the following year. He immediately resumed his terrible work, and it is estimated that he had some fifty heretics burned at the stake in a mad tour of Châlons-sur-Marne, Cambrai, Péronne, Douai, and Lille. Then, in 1239, at Mont-Aimé (in Champagne), according to an eyewitness, Aubri de Trois-Fontaines, it was this appalling stake that gathered together 183 victims following a

[7] *Bougre* (meaning brute or fellow) is a distortion of Bulgarian; it is possible, although not absolutely proven, that Catharism originated from Bogomile sects in Bulgarian regions where Manichaean (which is to say, dualist) doctrines were propagated (an evil god at the origin of the visible creation, opposed to the good god who created minds and spirits).

gigantic round-up at the time of the Provins trade fairs.[8]
Robert le Bougre was then, certainly from 1241 on, deprived of his office. He may have been condemned himself
to life imprisonment, but that has not been established as a
fact.

The Inquisition was equally severe in the south: and at
times quite drastically, as at Carcassonne, where, between 1237
and 1244, the inquisitor Ferrier acquired the surname "Ham-
mer of Heretics". Guillaume de Puylaurens, whose information is generally accurate, speaks of two hundred heretics
burned at the stake at Montségur in 1244, after the forced
surrender of the château where they had taken refuge from
the murderers of the Avignonnet inquisitor; many inaccu-
racies abound, actually, about this "stake at Montségur", which
has aroused in our time a vast literature of which not much
of historical value remains, especially after the works of Yves
Dossat.[9] On the other hand, much is known about the stake
at Berlaigues near Agen, where, shortly before his death, in
1249, the count of Toulouse, Raymond VII, had some eight
heretics burned.

It is pointless to become bogged down with the exagger-
ations about the Inquisition in works of imaginative writers
with little respect for documentary sources. The penalties
generally applied were "immuring", or imprisonment (there
was a distinction between the "narrow wall", which was prison
properly speaking, and the "large wall", which was a residence under surveillance), or, still more often, condemnation

---

[8] The Cathars in fact recruited their followers particularly from among merchants. They were accused, and, it seems, not without reason, of practicing
usury, that is, taking interest (the name "lombards", which was given them,
also meant usurers, that is, bankers).

[9] See no. 6, *Le Credo, la Morale et l'Inquisition*, particularly 361–78, in the
*Cahiers de Fanjeaux* previously cited.

to pilgrimages or to wearing a cloth cross sewn on one's garments. In places where their registers have survived, such as at Toulouse in 1245–1246, one notes that the inquisitors[10] pronounced a sentence to prison in one case out of nine on the average, to pain of fire in one case out of twenty, the other accused being either released or sentenced to lesser penalties.

That, however, is not the question. The disapproval of the Inquisition noticeable ever since the eighteenth century constitutes one of those advances that the historian cannot fail to stress, since it is raised against the very principle of judgments borne in the name of the faith; faith seems to us, in its very essence, to defy any pressure, any constraint of the external and juridical order.

In fact, for the believer—and the immense majority were believers in the Middle Ages—the Church is perfectly within her right in exercising a power of jurisdiction: insofar as she is guardian of the faith, this right has always been recognized in her by those who, by their baptism, belong to the Church. That was the reason, for example, for the general acceptance of sanctions such as excommunication or interdict. To excommunicate is to place outside the communion of the faithful the one who does not conform to the rules instituted by the Church as society; it is a "putting out of bounds", like that practiced everywhere for the one who cheats, betrays, who does not accept the rules of a society, a club, a party, any association whatever to which, moreover, one claims to belong. In the same line of ecclesiastical sanctions, interdict struck with a kind of general excommunication a whole territory, a whole town, in order to constrain to obedience the one who was responsible for it: the lord, king, even abbot,

[10] Ibid., 370ff.

and so on. This kind of outlawing by the society of the faithful was the most efficacious way to obtain the amendment of the guilty, for interdict caused the suspension of any religious ceremony; bells ceased to ring, services (marriages, burials . . .) were no longer celebrated, which made life literally intolerable for the people.

Nevertheless, the war against the southern heretics and the institution of the Inquisition clearly stand out against these ecclesiastical sanctions in that they involve recourse to force, to temporal power, to the "secular arms". It was an unusual thing in the Church, a new tendency that the canonists of the fourteenth and fifteenth centuries tried to justify and lay down as law, and which would have serious developments in the sixteenth century. The popes to whom these two measures are owing were those regarded very generally in history textbooks as the "great popes of the Middle Ages": Innocent III and Gregory IX. They were both—and it is important to note this—passionately interested in Roman law. It is well known how the rebirth of Roman law and its study, particularly at the university of Bologne, would gradually penetrate Church law—not as totally as they penetrated civil society afterward, in the seventeenth century and later, but nevertheless in a profound manner; under this influence, the "decretists", those employed with canon law, were on their way toward an authoritarian form of thought, toward the exercise of a centralized sovereignty.[11]

Now, despite the absolute clarity of the gospel about the separation of powers, Innocent III and Gregory IX both had

[11] Roman law, such as it was constituted, notably in the Eastern empire, with all the prestige conferred on it by the personality of Justinian, sprang from a unique and centralized authority and consequently formed customs and minds to the exercise of a similar authority, in the spiritual realm as in the temporal.

recourse to the temporal in order to preserve the spiritual. In other words, they opted for facility; and never perhaps in the course of history has the easy solution been better revealed for what it is: not a solution, but an open door to new and formidable problems.

Of course, they were not able to evaluate the consequences of their decisions, which were dictated by impatience, by a search for immediate efficacy—perfectly contrary to the spirit of the gospel—but also, more subtly, by this tendency toward authoritarianism that inevitably develops with the practice of Roman law. If both, moreover, had strong personalities, the sincerity of their religious zeal was nonetheless unquestionable: Innocent III was the one who was able to discern, in the midst of a multitude of very dissimilar tendencies aiming to lead to evangelical poverty a Church with a most pressing need for it, the authentic zeal of people like Domingo de Guzmán and Francis of Assisi; as for Gregory IX, it would not be an exaggeration to see him as a veritable champion of freedom of spirit: 1231, which was when he instituted the Inquisition, was also the year of the bull *Parens scientiarum*, by which he confirmed and formulated the privileges of the University of Paris and assured its independence with respect to the king and also the bishops and their chancellors; in short, he defined and recognized the freedom of philosophical and scientific research. He thus put an end to two years of troubles and strikes by the Paris masters and students in opposition to Queen Blanche of Castile and to her young son Louis IX by ungraciously obliging the latter to reestablish intact the privileges that shielded the universities from the very justice of the king.

Here we see an obvious example of the ambiguities of history, when, contrary to the image with which one is so often presented, it is very difficult to distinguish between the "good" and the "bad".

The institution of the Inquisition itself was not without its positive side in the concrete reality of life. It substituted the procedure of inquiry for the procedure of accusation. But above all, at a time when the people were not disposed to trifle with heretics, it introduced regular justice. For previously, it was in many cases a secular justice or even an outburst of the people that inflicted the worst suffering on heretics. It suffices to recall that King Robert the Pious had, in 1022, burned at the stake in Orléans fourteen heretics, clerics as well as laypeople. Moreover, in many circumstances, the bishops had had to intervene to shield those considered heretics from mob violence. Peter Abelard had experience of this, since he himself, at Soissons, in 1121, had been hit by stones thrown by an angry crowd. Several years before, heretics condemned to prison by the bishop of the same city of Soissons had been taken from it and led to the stake by rioters who reproached the bishop for his "priestly softness". At various times acts of violence had thus been committed, and it is known that, under Philip Augustus himself, eight Cathars had been burned at Troyes in the year 1200, while a little later, in 1209, the king inflicted the same punishment on several disciples of Amalric of Bena. In the south, at Saint-Gilles-du-Gard, the heretic Pierre de Bruys, who had publicly burned a crucifix, had the same punishment inflicted on him by a furious crowd.

It was perhaps inevitable that one day or another regular tribunals would be instituted, but these tribunals were marked by a particular harshness due to the renaissance of Roman law: the constitutions of Justinian in fact ordered heretics put to death. And it was in order to revive these constitutions that Frederick II, who had become emperor of Germany, promulgated in 1224 new imperial constitutions that, for the first time, stipulated specifically the pain of fire against hardened heretics. Thus the Inquisition, at its most odious, was the fruit of dispositions made at its beginning by an emperor recognized as the forerunner of the "enlightened monarch", who was, moreover, himself a skeptic and soon excommunicated.

Consequently, in adopting the punishment of burning at the stake, in instituting as a legal procedure recourse to the "secular arm" for the relapsed,[12] the pope was strengthening even more the effect of imperial legislation and was officially recognizing the rights of the temporal power in pursuit of heresy. Still under the influence of imperial legislation, torture would be officially authorized—when there had been some beginning of proof—in the middle of the thirteenth century.

Now, all this legislative apparatus against heresy was not long in being turned back by that same temporal power against the spiritual power of the pope. Under Philip the Fair, accusations against Boniface VIII, against Bernard Saisset, against the Knights Templar, against Guichard de Troyes, rested on this recognized power of the king to pursue heretics. More than ever, the confusion between spiritual and temporal played to the benefit of the latter. We do not have to recall here the final consequences: the Inquisition of the sixteenth century, henceforth entirely in the hands of kings and emperors, would make the number of victims rise completely out of proportion to those of the thirteenth century. In Spain, they would go so far as to use the Inquisition against the Jews and Moors, which amounted to diverting it completely from its purpose.

---

[12] The *relaps*, or relapsed, was a hardened heretic, one who, having abjured the first time, fell back into his error; only this "relapsed" heretic could be remitted to the "secular arms"—a modest expression to signify that the temporal authority had been charged with taking him to burn at the stake.

In fact, it was supposed to be, if one may say so, for internal use: intended to detect heretics, that is, those who, belonging to the Church, were turning against her. Thus, in the thirteenth century, Ferdinand III, king of Spain (cousin of Saint Louis, he would also be canonized), had refused the Inquisition: there were no heretics in his kingdom, and he proclaimed himself "king of three religions": (Christian, Jewish, and Muslim)—which implied a wholly different state of mind than what we see during the period of Charles V and Philip II!

Moreover, when we speak of confusion between the spiritual and the temporal, it is necessary to have an understanding of dates and periods. When, in the twelfth century, a "benefice"—the yield from land—was given to any curate or prelate whatever, it was a question of assuring his material life, land being at that time the sole source of wealth. The pontifical domain itself had no other object but to supply the living of the bishop of Rome and his advisers, the cardinals who surrounded him. In the course of the thirteenth century, under the influence of Roman law and in great part because of conflicts with the emperor, the pontiff became a head of state; this evolution was confirmed, in any case in intention if not in fact, when Boniface VIII added a third crown to his tiara: that which symbolized precisely his temporal power (we know that the pontifical tiara appeared only in the course of the thirteenth century; it carried one, then two crowns, which, like the two keys, signified the double power of order and of jurisdiction that belongs to all bishops).

For the preceding epoch (seven and one-half centuries out of the ten centuries of the Middle Ages!), those who imagine a monolithic Church wielding an absolute power in the person of the pope are radically contradicted by the facts: let us recall that, in the twelfth and thirteenth centuries (out of two hundred years, then), the popes had to reside *122* years outside of Rome, living as outlaws and exiles, chased by factions and revolts that continuously fed the history of Rome.

The character of power proper to the papacy in the feudal period was never better expressed in reality than when, at the Council of Clermont, Urban II decided what the first crusade[13] in 1095 was to be called: the pope, who was coming at that time to exhort the Christians to reconquer the holy places invaded by the Turks, was a wanderer, chased out of Rome; when he opened the council, he began by excommunicating the king of France from the kingdom where he happened to be, in defiance of the most elementary diplomatic precautions; impotent in his own territory, he nonetheless unleashed a movement that would permit Christianity to recover what it considered to be its own fief and the very site of its pilgrimage.

Very different would be the preoccupations of Boniface VIII, imbued with as much authoritarian power as Philip the Fair and who himself adopted an attitude of a head of state. Then the true confusion between spiritual power and temporal power would begin. The popes, who had been able, thanks to the Gregorian reform, to disengage themselves from the hold of the emperor, would fall under the control of the king of France for nearly a century. They would free themselves of it only at the price of a schism that would weigh on the Church for nearly a half-century; the confusion between the powers would be consummated with the Concordat of Bologne (1516), which, in France, would place all nomina-

---

[13] Let us recall that the word "crusade" is modern and was never pronounced at that time; they said: pilgrimage, passage, voyage, or overseas expedition.

tions of abbots and bishops back in the hands of the king, the temporal power. Even today we do not calculate the true cost of these four centuries of a functionary church, for the effects of the Concordat of 1516 were prolonged in France up to the 1904 law of separation: four hundred years of a state church during which all the bishops and all the abbots of monasteries were named by the king and then the heads of state, even if they were, as was Jules Ferry, confirmed anticlerics.

It is only just barely at the end of our own twentieth century that the general mentality (of nonbelievers as well as believers) has in fact been freed from habits of mind modeled by the state church—a centralized, authoritarian church with structures guaranteed by the temporal power, that of the state whatever its form. The result, in the seventeenth century, was the superb façade of religion, with its sermons, set in grand opera decor, gathering together the court and the great around the pulpit; the easily guaranteed docility of the prelates matched the licentiousness flaunted by some of them, even archbishops like the one of Reims, Maurice Le Tellier, brother of Louvois, who paraded his mistresses in state, one of whom was his own niece, and so forth; and, on the other hand, in the face of this glitter—that of buildings and hierarchical structure—the disaffection with contemplative life increased, as witnessed by the spiritual decay of the abbeys (there were five monks at Cluny when the Revolution broke out!).[14]

There is no need to dwell on this: the profound improprieties, inseparable from a state church, were manifest up to

[14] The history of the order of Grandmont is very characteristic. Founded in Limousin in the twelfth century, it had been comprised in France of 160 houses. It counted no more than nine religious when it was suppressed in 1780. See the study devoted to it by André Lanthonie, *Histoire de l'abbaye de Grandmont en Limousin* (Saint-Yrieux-la-Perche: Imp. Fabrègue, 1976).

a time very close to our own in some countries.[15] In the history of the Church of France nothing less than the ascetical holiness of reforms like those of the Carmelites and Trappists was necessary in order to keep the Church alive beneath her magnificent and ridiculous exterior. In signing the Concordat, the pope (Leo X, a Medici, the same one who responded to the protestations of Luther by excommunicating him) did, it is true, reserve a right of veto in ecclesiastical nominations: a veto he *never* used. Henry IV was able to name as bishop a child of six months, and that same Maurice Le Tellier, already named, would be abbot of Lagny at nine years of age. Thus, the very thing that had constituted abuse, illegitimate favor, exception—the nomination of bishops or abbots by the favor of the seignorial or royal power—during the whole of the medieval period (with the exception of the Carolingian interlude) became at the beginning of the sixteenth century *the* law.

It is curious to note that these facts, which are so evident, so easy to find out in the history of the West, are very generally ignored, misunderstood, passed over in silence, or inaccurately appreciated, particularly by the clergy and Catholic press.

To come back to the Inquisition,[16] its creation helped, in the eyes of the historian, to make the Church, and in general the West, evolve toward that fanatic form taken by religious

[15] Moreover, it was everywhere that the Churches fell under the domination of the temporal power, in Protestant countries like Sweden, Denmark, England, Germany, and even Switzerland as well as in the Catholic countries, which, following the example of France, concluded concordats attributing to princes or emperors the power to nominate dignitaries. It is then that we can speak of confusion between the spiritual and the temporal, a confusion that was translated into a complete subjection of Church structures, henceforth confused with those of the state.

[16] For the believer, it would be rather reassuring to note that none of the "great popes"—Innocent III and Gregory IX—was canonized by the Church; on the contrary, it was Louis IX who was canonized; he was born, let us recall, five years after the launching of the Albigensian war and was fifteen years old

expression in the sixteenth century at precisely the time of the wars of religion. The face of the Church became at that time effectively monolithic, tied to the state and to a whole, purely Western bureaucracy and mentality. Having ceased to experience the perpetual reforms that had constituted her life up until then, she saw *the* Reformation put into action against her. In fact, in order to let this all sink in, one need only compare this rigidity to the efforts made in the twelfth century to know and understand the non-Christian currents she was facing; one need only call to mind someone like Peter the Venerable, abbot of Cluny, having the Talmud and the Koran translated in 1141 (is it well known that, subsequently, it was obligatory for *all* preachers of the crusades to have read the Koran?) in order to appreciate the difference between that and the evangelization of the seventeenth and following centuries, which has been reproached, and not without reason, for its narrowly "Western" character. The Church of the fifth and sixth centuries had known how to "get through to the barbarians"; she had actively distributed instruction among these "barbarians" as among the heirs of the culture of antiquity—whereas when she evangelized South America, she completely neglected this instruction, which would have assured her own increase in that land. Wherever evangelization, whether Protestant or Catholic, appeared in the classical period, moreover, it remained the servant of the West.[17] It is startling to think that at the end of the thirteenth

when the latter ended with the peace treaty of 1229; he was seventeen years old at the time when the Inquisition (which he would support in his domains) was created; the Church also canonized his cousin, Ferdinand III, who refused to admit the Inquisition into Spain.

[17] It was difficult, besides, to reconcile the concerns for evangelization with the various forms of oppression in force: slavery in the Antilles, genocide in North America and Australia . . .

century, there was in China a thriving Christianity grouping six dioceses around the archbishop of Peking. The subjection of the papacy by the temporal power, the disorders that such a situation inevitably entails, even if only in favoring the appetite for riches and honors, led in the fourteenth century to a nearly complete disinterest in this church of the Far East, whose existence would resume only several centuries later. These are a few facts that should be kept in mind when one pronounces (and, God knows, one does pronounce them!) judgments about what is conventionally called the "Church of the Middle Ages".

Someone will undoubtedly call my attention to the fact that this is only one instance among many others of that accusing finger that is raised so often and so freely in our period to denounce evil, scandal, corruption, deviation, and so on (courageously, for it is understood that denunciation is invariably an act of courage). It is remarkable that the Evil is always situated directly in front of the one who points the finger, who, himself, inevitably, personifies the Good. One might wonder if the Manichaean doctrines that gave rise to the Inquisition—and, moreover, influenced to some degree the inquisitors themselves!—had not thoroughly penetrated the mentality even of our own times.

There would obviously be many other things to say on this subject. I am thinking of that young friend, full of ardor and a militant CFDT,[18] who explained to me with much conviction that the Church today had finally understood that to serve one's neighbor was to serve God and that this overwhelming discovery in the history of Christianity was going to change completely the basic relational experience, indeed, the whole of socio-cultural behavior in the Christian milieu. I asked her

[18] The CFDT is one of France's three largest trade unions.—TRANS.

how a simple mind like mine could account for the reason that led the Christians of the Middle Ages to call the "Hôtel Dieu", or "Maison-Dieu", not the churches, but the places where they received and cared free of charge for the poor, the sick, and those in misery, and if that did not have some connection to what she was calling the relational experience? Her response probably exceeded the capacities of a simple mind, for I do not remember any of it any more.

I could have reminded her, too, how the statutes of the hospitalier orders prescribed receiving the sick, whoever they were and wherever they came from, "as if they were the lord of the house". Or, too, I might have mentioned the right of sanctuary, which perhaps would be useful to revive on a large scale in an era when the spirit of public and private vengeance has also been reborn. But I was not sure that my young militant would have heard me to the end, and, besides, I was vaguely uneasy, wondering what judgment she would unfailingly bring to bear on the way in which Joinville understood the relational experience.

* * *

A television broadcast had been devoted in 1970 to the International Red Cross and its investigating commissions in internment camps. Its representative was questioned by various people, among them a journalist who asked the question: "Can one not *oblige* countries to accept the investigating commission of the Red Cross?"

And as the representative of this institution remarked that the investigating commissions had no other means at their disposal except to have their observations recorded, observed, or sanctioned, and that, besides, these commissions themselves were not enjoined by a right of visitation admitted and recognized by all, the same journalist resumed: "Can

civilized nations not then ban those who refuse your investigating commissions?"

In listening to this dialogue with reference to history, one
could say to oneself that in her indignation, which was certainly understandable, this journalist had just successively
invented the Inquisition, excommunication, and interdict—
except that she was applying them to a domain where agreement was unanimous, that of protection of political prisoners
and interned persons.

But there is no need to go looking for comparisons of this
kind. What period better than ours can understand the medieval Inquisition, if only we transpose the offensive opinion
from the religious domain to the political? It is even very
surprising for the historian to note this rise of severity per-
vading all countries toward the offensive political opinion.
All exclusion, all punishment, all slaughter seems justified in
our times in order to punish or forestall deviations or errors
relating to the political line adopted by the powers that be.
And in most cases, it is not enough to banish the one who
succumbs to political heresy; it is important to convince.
Whence we have brainwashing and interminable imprisonment that wear down man's capacity for inner resistance.
When one thinks of the appalling total, of the insane expen-
diture in human lives—worse even than that of the two "world
wars"—by which the successive revolutions and the punishment of differences of opinion in our twentieth century have
been carried out, one can wonder if in this domain of dif-
fering opinions the notion of progress has not been checked.
For the historian of the year 3000, where will fanaticism lie?
Where, the oppression of man by man? In the thirteenth
century or the twentieth?

8

# HISTORY, IDEAS, AND FANTASY

A young man of the overly excitable but likeable sort appeared at my office in the National Archives one day wanting to give me (I still wonder why) a biography he had written about the all-too-famous Cathars. Skimming through a few pages led me to ask him about his background as a historian; it turned out that, in fact, he had not spent much time looking into authentic sources. Which provoked an indignant outburst: "You must understand, when I do history, it is not in order to know if some particular fact is accurate or not; I am looking for what can promote my ideas."

That necessitated my reply: "Then, dear sir, why do you do history? Turn to politics, novels, film, journalism! History is of interest only when it is a search for truth; it ceases to be *history* the moment it becomes something else." He left disappointed and, it seems, extremely irritated.

At least he was honest in his reactions concerning it. That is not always so common. The Middle Ages furnishes a choice field to all those for whom history is only a pretext: a period about which the public at large is ignorant, with a few recognizable names: Charlemagne, Joan of Arc, the Inquisition, the Cathars, the *Chanson de Roland*, the troubadours, the Knights Templar, Abelard, the *Grail*, feudal, which rhymes with brutal, and serfs busy making the frogs keep quiet. That is very nearly the average stock of knowledge delivered by textbooks for elementary education. If one wishes to spice it up a bit, one can add the secret of the Templars and the treasure of the Cathars, or, inversely, the secret of the Cathars and the treasure of the Templars. In return for which, one can "promote ideas" supremely well, as my young interlocutor wished. And it is done generally with an ease that always surprises us, we poor ones, for whom history is the patient study of often very dry but always concrete documents, traces of events lived by living persons, and who are little concerned to submit to prefabricated theories or obey predetermined statistics.

It is probably one of the major errors of our time: this belief that history is created in our little brains, that one can construct it "at will". The attitude of that writer (the director of a "history series"—what a shame!) who, in a discussion about the origins of Christopher Colombus, said to the historian Marianne Mahn-Lot: "Your thesis is perhaps true, but leave people free to think as they wish!" is perfectly typical. It would undoubtedly have embarrassed this gentleman to be asked the time. If he had responded "8:30 P.M.", one could have retorted: "Leave me free to think as I wish: I think it's three in the morning."

It would be impossible to deny history more ingenuously or more brazenly. The freedom of thought that history, like all scientific research, implies and necessitates can in no way be confused with the intellectual fantasies of an individual, dictated by his political options, his personal opinions, or his impulses of the moment, or more simply by the desire to write a big book with a large edition. History has its proper domain. It ceases to exist if it is no longer a search for the true, founded on authentic documents; it literally evaporates; at best it is only fraud and mystification. This is the place to cite the very fine definition by Henri-Irénée Marrou: "A man of science, the historian is, as it were, delegated by his fellow men to the conquest of truth." [1]

Someone will raise in objection the great successes of historical literature; but precisely when someone like Shakespeare recreates Henri V, he does so by respecting the truth of the person, so that history is revealed to us. Much more debatable is someone like Walter Scott, imposing an image of Louis XI that has nothing in common with the Louis XI of history—even if that image has managed to slip even into scholarly textbooks! Finally, we have what we see every day: borrowing the names of historical personages to pass off productions that have nothing in common, unfortunately, with the works of Shakespeare or even of Walter Scott, merely pitiful counterfeits destined to abuse the good people they scorn. With their eyes on the taste for history that the public is increasingly showing (a healthy reflex in an era of cheap philosophies, purely abstract systems, and merely intellectual, notional, cerebral theories, and so on), writers hastily adopt a few familiar names (Christopher Colombus, Joan of Arc, and so on), a few themes already known to trigger a political resonance (the Cathars, the Templars . . .), in return for which they build a "historical" work, indeed a whole, "very saleable" series, enlarging on the subject with a few mini-scandals according to proven journalistic methods.

It is so easy, in fact, to manipulate history, consciously or unconsciously, for a public that is not knowledgeable about it. We have nearly daily evidence of this on television. When the events recounted are so recent that their distortion on screen can be corrected, there is only minimal harm done.

---

[1] *De la connaissance historique* (Paris: Éd. du Seuil, 1954), 219. (There was a new edition of this title in 1975).

But for an author to attack (and that is the appropriate word) the Albigensian question, for example, how many would be in a position to protest? He can blithely bring to life someone like Saint Dominic some twenty years older than he was, confuse that person with some other, and compose a tissue of errors that leaves the specialist amazed. The latter would have no other resource but a critique that would remain nearly private in some learned journal. The Middle Ages is privileged material: one can say what one wants about it with the quasi-certitude of never being contradicted.

So, too, the life of the medievalist could be consumed with redressing errors, for nearly always the facts, the texts of the time, contradict the legends accumulated ever since the sixteenth century and spread particularly since the nineteenth. It is very rare to begin a subject without having first to straighten out the fables to which it has given rise. To restrict myself to one very characteristic example, although drawn from recent history and not from the Middle Ages, I experienced this very thing not long ago (1974) under conditions that might have been considered exemplary. A scriptwriter had called on me at the National Archives, looking for documentation concerning the attempt made by Damiens against Louis XV. The scriptwriter had at first asked to see the parliamentary record "from which the pages had been torn out". In fact, all historians since Michelet—more accurately, since Ravaisson, who preceded him—have recounted that the pages containing the parliamentary deliberations on the Damiens affair had been torn out; now, on inspection of the authentic record, we have been able to ascertain that the latter is in fine condition and quite complete, that the pages follow each other in their original order of pagination, faultlessly, and that the deliberations are recounted at full length, without detectable addition or subtraction. Michelet also wrote that the object produced in evidence in this trial remained "only one poor red rag", Damiens' shirt; in fact the collection in the National Archives of the objects produced in evidence for the state trial preserves intact, although very moth-eaten, Damiens' entire outfit—simple for the period but, being of admirably woven pure wool, carefully sewn and decorated, it would be for our time a true masterpiece of great tailoring, with waistcoat, jabot, one glove, and so on.

The error, in fact, is easily discernible: it stems from a first "historian" who repeated court gossip according to which Damiens' attempt was supposedly, as we would say, guided by high-placed personages who would have wished their names hidden from the deliberations. A mere fable, totally unfounded, which the state of the registers, like the records—everything, once again, absolutely complete without the least thing missing—contradicts. Now, Michelet, when he wrote the second part of his *Histoire de France*, that is to say, the monarchical period up to the Revolution (he wrote *L'Histoire de la Révolution* at an earlier date), had been far removed from the National Archives for nearly twenty years: the prince-president had withdrawn him from the post he had occupied there because of his refusal to preach him a sermon in 1852. He thus wrote the chapter concerning Damiens on the basis of some very vague personal memories—the "poor red shirt"—and on the basis of an earlier historian, a bad choice, under the circumstances. This is not the only occasion where we find, in the last part of his work, information of a quality far inferior to that of the first part, written before the events of 1848–1852.

Consequently, with respect to Damiens' attempt, it was necessary first of all, with the documents in hand, to correct the initial inaccuracy that falsified the whole history of the trial of that unfortunate—a half-crazy victim of a penal procedure that became one of unimaginable cruelty in the seventeenth and eighteenth centuries.

A typical anecdote, an error easy to rectify because it was a question of relatively recent history. For the Middle Ages, errors of the same kind abound; they often stem from the fact that people neglect to go back to the sources.

I would recall here one revealing example, and one that this time takes us right back to the Middle Ages. All those who, in our time, have visited Rocamadour have heard about a Saint Amadour, who was none other than Zachaeus, the publican from the Gospel, converted by Christ, who, coming to evangelize the Gauls, supposedly died as a hermit in these mountains, to which he gave his name, whence Roc Amadour.

Having had to study, in preparation for a congress, the *Livre des Miracles de Notre-Dame de Rocamadour*, whose original manuscript from the twelfth century has been preserved, I was able to ascertain that there was absolutely no question of either Zachaeus or any Saint Amadour whatever, all the miracles reported having been attributed explicitly to Christ, on the intercession of the Virgin. From a more attentive study, it was evident that the legend goes back to the fifteenth century (three hundred years after the *Livre des Miracles* was written); it is explicitly recounted only in a literary work that appeared in 1633; finally, it was admitted into the liturgy only around 1850, in the middle of the nineteenth century. Hundreds of anecdotes like this could be recounted.

Go back to the sources, but not to any sources whatever, for confusion between literary sources and historical sources is very common. Obviously, when one takes literally, as of the "first order", the content of the *chansons de geste* or that of the chivalric novels and tries to make their characters into examples drawn from current life, the humanity one describes is peopled with monsters, enormities, aberrations. Simple good sense should be enough, it would seem, to rectify errors of this kind. Nothing of the sort. I have seen commentators, in France especially, persist in taking literally works of pure phantasmagoria. All one can ask of a literary work is to be a reflection of a mentality, not the description of a reality, still less its exact description. The nineteenth century saw the blossoming of a new genre with the naturalistic novel; yet one would be completely mistaken if one took Père Goriot or Lucien de Rubempré to be historical personages. Nevertheless that is precisely what some have done with respect to *Raoul de Cambrai*, for example; and yet, the epic, like the chivalric novel, is radically different, in its very essence, from the naturalistic novel: the author is no more concerned to copy reality than the sculptor who fashions the characters on a Roman capital. In spite of that, one has drawn from *Raoul de Cambrai* the prototype of a pillaging, ravaging, unjust, and cruel lord: it would have been more advisable to look for a prototype in chronicles, and still more so in documents like cartularies or others things of that kind. But it is easier to embroider all facts eternally on the same schemes rather than study donations, leases, acts of sale and exchange, and so forth. That, however, is where history is found, not in literature.

All this goes to say that, in order to know a millennium of our history, an immense effort remains to be made on the historical, which is the scientific, level, by avoiding reference to some vague folklore fed by never-ceasing chronicles, indeed, merely by earlier studies, going back to the eighteenth or nineteenth century and necessarily incomplete or of inaccurate interpretation. It is enough to remember the person of Abelard, who has been made out to be an unbeliever, a lost skeptic in a century of ignorance and degradation. Trying to pass off as a skeptic the thinker whose every effort of thought was devoted to establishing the dogma of the Holy Trinity, the theologian who cleared the way for Thomas Aquinas himself, is in itself rather paradoxical; this is, however, what one reads nearly everywhere in popular works.

The only one of Abelard's works that has been translated is the famous and wonderful *Lettre à une ami*, as well as his correspondence with Héloïse.[2] His philosophical work remains practically ignored, except by specialists who have read the Latin text. I personally had a rather curious misadventure with respect to it: After looking through many others, I opened up his *Historia* in a series in which marginal notes had been used to clarify difficult terms, a practice excellent in itself. These notes had been written by a history *agregé*.[3]

Now, I was greatly surprised to note the liberties that this annotator had taken with the texts of Abelard himself, particularly with *Sic et non*, the work that has been used more than any other to make him out to be a skeptic. The annotator had inserted some comments drawn from current textbooks: the result was very surprising—to say the least—for anyone who had taken the trouble to read the whole of *Sic et non* itself. If he had merely read the wonderful prologue, which indicates the intention of the rest of the work (which is composed essentially of quotations from Scripture and the Fathers of the Church), his comments would have been quite

---

[2] A translation into English of his *Éthique* has been made by the scholar D. E. Luscombe (Oxford: Clarendon Press, 1971).

[3] Let us remember that the *agrégation* [an examination for admission to teaching positions in higher education] forms, not historians, which is to say researchers working on original texts, but professors of history—which is not the same thing.

different. And this is why the image of Abelard that appears in his writings differs to such a degree from the one fabricated and spread by historians of the eighteenth and nineteenth centuries (at a time when his work had been only partially published), which well-educated readers wrongly believe until the authentic texts are quoted to them. The most striking example is undoubtedly that of Saint Louis, the least known of the kings of France. It is extraordinary to think that the complete catalogue of the acts of Saint Louis has not yet been drawn up, although such catalogues have been compiled for the kings who preceded him and for those who followed him; perhaps the excessive number of documents that survive a reign that covered more than forty years of our history has discouraged scholars. From all evidence, such a work would necessitate a team; now chartists, who are admirably trained in the study of historical documents, are in very short supply for such teamwork. We thus know Saint Louis only through chroniclers—very well informed and at times endowed with immense talent, like Joinville—who allow us to grasp his personality, but we continue to have no knowledge of or to know only approximately his true work, the acts of his public and private life; and, we might say, we have only secondhand knowledge of his reign. To emphasize the gaps in our information, let us point out that we still do not have a critical edition of Joinville's work itself; endlessly edited and reedited, it is always only according to the old edition of Natalis de Wailly; there is no question of an edition answering the present need of establishing a text according to existing manuscripts. Thus our knowledge of Saint Louis' reign has not gone beyond the level of historical synthesis, on which we continue to rely: the work of Le Nain de Tillemont, composed in the seventeenth century but edited only a century later by Jules de Gaulle for the Société de l'Histoire de France—while the most valuable chronicle concerning that reign has still not received the attention it merits.

Another example, in a very different domain, was pointed out by a recent thesis.[4] We know that only a fraction of Stephen Langton's work has been published: precisely one sermon out of nearly three hundred, one biblical commentary, although he wrote a commentary for all the books of the Bible, and a single *quaestio* out of seventy have been made available to us. The public at large does not even know the name of Stephen Langton. But in order to appreciate this lacuna, one must know that all those, from the thirteenth century up to our time, who have quoted some particular passage of the Bible with its reference (which represents several million or even billions of citations) owe something to the work of this person, who fixed, even for our time, the *capitulation* of the Bible, its division into chapters and verses, which even the Jewish Bible has adopted. That is enough to express the importance of the one who, after graduation from the University of Paris, was archbishop of Canterbury and also played a decisive role in the drafting of the English Magna Carta in 1215.

Work is certainly not lacking to future generations of historians of the Middle Ages, but some courage will be required of them in order to carry it out, and also some independence of mind and spirit. We have often enough received the confidences of graduate students preparing for their *agrégation* examination to know how concerned we must be on this subject: those who want to do a master's thesis on the

---

[4] Amaury d'Esneval, *L'Inspiration biblique d'Étienne Langton à travers le commentaire sur le livre de Ruth et les "Interpretationes nominum hebraicorum"* (doctoral thesis, University of Caen, 1976).

history of the Middle Ages have, with very rare exceptions, been discouraged by professors and future thesis readers whom they consulted. Not that deceptive motives need be supposed in these people: simply, and most seriously, they did not have the necessary competence, and even less curiosity. So we arrive at this paradox: those who are studying the history of Greek and Roman antiquity and even Byzantine antiquity have all kinds of difficulties finding subjects for theses and doctoral dissertations because the questions have already been studied and excavated in every nook and cranny, while those who would like to move toward our own history, where enormous gaps, true abysses remain to be filled, find themselves diverted.

The same holds true in all fields, not just history properly speaking: the history of people and events but also the history of philosophy, that of ideas, social history, the history of human groups, the history of customs, that of law . . . The result is this quasi-absolute void one encounters on these various questions in general works, encyclopedias, world histories, and so on, where the medieval period is treated in a few pages—a thousand years polished off!—in total disproportion to all other periods, including the ancient period. Whatever the questions considered, these thousand years are blithely passed over. Very characteristic was the attitude of that philosopher who, while loudly proclaiming his scorn for those at the Sorbonne, the University, and so on, nonetheless adopted with rare docility of mind the most absolute dogma of the Sorbonne in this matter, since he treated these thousand years in five or six pages in a *Histoire de la philosophie*. "For the Sorbonne, there was nothing between Plotinus and Descartes", a young student preparing for his *agrégation* observed to me—one of those who, persuaded precisely that something must have gone on in the domain of thought between Plotinus and Descartes, would have liked to take an interest in it himself.

Is that a scientific position? Is it even, quite simply, an intelligent position?

There will undoubtedly be a number of objections. Great names can be cited, scholarly journals, centers of medieval studies like the one at Poitiers, several congresses, seminars, and even some university courses, such as the course in medieval iconography at Mans. All that exists, but it does not invalidate the rule. The rule is that the student in literature does a thesis on Proust, and the student of history agrees to be interested in everything except the medieval period.

At least that was so up until very recently. One senses today a growing interest that might, after all, be capable of breaking open the doors of the University. Modern means of exploiting documents could allow a renewed and extended study of them. Information processing is penetrating the Archives; it is destined to render immense services. Undoubtedly it will be applied more to later periods, for it is very rare to possess for the feudal period whole groups of extensive and complete enough documents for there to be interest in handling them by data processing; some categories, however, would lend themselves to it. Consider, for example, the surveys of Saint Louis and all they might reveal to us about the social life of the time. For the later period, the parish registers (we know that the oldest ones in France go back to the fourteenth century) have already been the subject of examination but even so, if certain specialists are to be believed, have not been thoroughly explored, for in setting up the programs, the godfathers and godmothers, whose roles were so important in the past, were overlooked; which is to say that no matter how perfect the means, they give their full yield, in history as elsewhere, only when they are conducted and used by already duly qualified researchers.

What could be developed prodigiously and is yet only in an embryonic state is the use of processes of reproduction to gain a better knowledge of our past. In particular the reproduction of the miniatures in manuscripts. That represents a practically limitless and almost unused resource with respect to what might be done. The image, the knowledge we have of the Middle Ages through architecture, sculpture, stained-glass windows, frescoes, even tapestries—"open air" documentation—represents not even a hundredth part of what we might learn from the reproduction of manuscript miniatures, if this were systematically carried out with the means of color reproduction we have available today. It is quite surprising that in the audio-visual era nothing has yet been undertaken in this sense on the requisite scale. A profound gap will remain in our knowledge of the Middle Ages as long as the necessary effort has not been carried out in this domain. For the moment, we always have to be content with nearly the same images, while manuscript illustrations, an incredibly rich source (we know that there are more than four thousand miniatures),[5] has remained stable (in contrast to what has happened with frescoes, whose colors have more or less faded or paled) and represent an immense panorama of interest not only to the history of art, properly speaking, but also to that of all social and economic life, and so forth. Only England has made an effort: the British Museum offers visitors a permanent exhibition of some two hundred manuscripts

[5] Let us cite the *Bible historiée* (Français 167 in the Bibliothèque nationale), which includes 5,152 images, the famous *Brévaire du duc de Bedford* (Latin 17, 294), which has 4,346 images, and so on. Even in manuscripts where the illuminated pages number in the dozens or hundreds, one must still add the marginal decorations, where are often very rich.

and, for those interested, provides terms of price and execution suited to the encouragement of reproductions; on
the other hand, private collections of photographs like the
Courtauld Institute allow a larger public to gain knowledge
of what in France might be considered an unexplored treasure, indispensable to the knowledge of the Middle Ages
and paradoxically less accessible than the results of archeological digs, which are generally never long in coming to
enrich museums.

* * *

In 1969, shortly after man's first steps on the moon, while
the television was questioning a group of children about the
reasons for the technical progress of mankind, a little boy
replied: "It is because *after* the Middle Ages, people began to
think!" He might have been eight or nine years old, but
already he knew that during the Middle Ages people did not
think.

I have already said this, but I must repeat that this ignorance is not the prerogative of young children, which would
of course be excusable, since they are repeating what they
have been taught. I recall the conversation I had with a Catholic television reporter. The subject was Joan of Arc's trial.
(*Le Monde* had published an article about a recent work on
Joan of Arc. Therefore, Catholic TV could, in turn, without
excessive risk, hazard to speak of her . . .).

This reporter who was interviewing me asked how the
acts of the trial were known, and I explained that we possessed the authentic account made by notaries—just as in
any juridical action of the period—of the questions posed
by the tribunal and the replies made by the accused.

"But, then, they wrote everything down?"

"Yes, everything."

"That must be a very big file?"

"Yes, very big."

I had the impression I was speaking with an illiterate. "Then, in order to publish it, there were people who re-copied everything?"

"Yes, everything."

And I could tell he was plunged into a stupefaction so intense that any insistence on the matter would have to be gentle; he murmured to himself: "It's hard to believe that *those people* could do things so carefully . . ."

"Those people . . . so carefully." It was my turn to be astonished: Had this journalist never looked at a Gothic arch? He had never asked himself if, in order to have it hang suspended for nearly a thousand years at some 130 feet from the ground, it might not have been necessary to make it carefully? He reminded me of that other interlocutor who—again with respect to Joan of Arc—said to me, quite haughtily: "You would really think that if documents from that period did still exist, they would have to be in such a condition that one couldn't read anything at all in them . . . !" Of course, in order to convince him, I would have had to invite him to come see some of the yards of shelving in the National Archives. He would immediately have recognized that parchment and rag paper are much tougher than our newsprint. But that is of little importance. What is at issue is this infantile vision of one part of mankind's history. There is a primary and decisive progress the needs to be made in what concerns the Middle Ages, which would be to admit that "those people" were people like us; a humanity like our own, neither better nor worse, but before whom it is not enough to shrug one's shoulders or smile condescendingly; one can study them as serenely as any other people.

That would obviously imply renouncing the term Middle Ages, at least in designating the whole of that millennium that separates antiquity from the Renaissance. If we admit that many things can happen in a period of over a thousand years, that should lead to, insofar as one holds to classifications (let us recognize that they do have their usefulness), a more differentiated nomenclature. Moreover, many scholars have already adopted one, and there is no reason for common knowledge to be so far behind scholarship in a time when considerable progress has been achieved precisely in the speed of communication. We could thus speak of a *Frank* period, during which what is called the High Middle Ages begins, designating the approximately three hundred years that run from the fall of the Roman Empire (410, if the point of departure chosen is the seizing of Rome by the Goths; 476, if it is the deposing of the last emperor) up to the accession of the Carolingian dynasty, in the middle of the eighth century. We would thus enclose a first phase, which no more deserves to be forgotten than those that precede and follow it. It represents, if one seeks an equivalent, a time equal to that which runs from the accession of Henry IV (1589) to the War of 1914.

A second section could be the *imperial* period: it saw the realization of a unified Europe, which is not of negligible interest in our twentieth century. It includes a period of about two hundred years: like the period from the death of Louis XV (1774) to our time (1975).

From the middle of the tenth century up to the end of the thirteenth century is the *feudal age*, which, itself, constitutes a unity, in France particularly, with common and strongly marked traits that characterize those three and a half centuries: the same stretch of time as between Joan of Arc (1429) and the French Revolution.

Finally, one could reserve the term *Middle Ages* for the last two centuries (the same interval as between the death of Louis XIV [1715] and the Soviet Revolution); that time was effectively a period of transition between feudalism and the monarchy, from the political point of view, with its violent social, economic, and even artistic changes.

We should note that for this last period—and it alone—the summary views of the Middle Ages as a period of wars, famines, and epidemics would be justified. It was precisely to improve these primitive chronologies that we set up, in the course of a colloquium with history students, the silhouette of the man of 1250, to which we contrasted that of the man of 1350. A fruitful confrontation between two worlds whose differences are radically apparent. In 1350, man in Europe had just been shaken by the most violent cataclysm he had ever known: the Bubonic plague, or the black death, which, as we know, appeared in 1347–1348[6] and touched no fewer than one man in three. Even so that estimate has turned out to be lower than the true number everywhere accurate figures have been possible to obtain. It suffices to recall that at Marseille, for example, the religious houses of Dominicans and Franciscans were entirely emptied, that some country villages were totally wiped off the map.

In France, the plague followed the battle of Crécy, which brought down, in 1346, according to the expression of the time, "the flower of French chivalry". Which is to say, the noble families, those at the very least of northern France, were literally decapitated. In addition, a new element had just transformed the conditions of war: gunpowder, which made its appearance on the battlefield in the first half of

[6] It had raged earlier in Europe, in the eighth century, and had not reappeared since.

the fourteenth century. Even if, under the conditions in which it was used, it caused more fear than evil, its use reversed the proportion between the means of defense and the means of attack; those who up until then were the weakest were about to become the strongest, and that created an entirely different mentality. If previously war was above all a matter of taking prisoners, now it was an attempt to kill the adversary. For some time yet, attention would still be paid to means of defense: it was the reason for which, in that fourteenth century, we see the appearance of the steel-clad knight, while in 1250 the warrior, who felt protected behind fortress walls and did not have to defend himself with firearms, was content with his coat of mail, with his helmet and leggings; in 1350, man himself became a moving fortress and, moreover, increasingly hindered in his movements, devoted himself above all to means of attack; the latter would never cease being perfected up to the time of the great slaughters with gas chambers and atomic bombs.

Recent studies have shown, in addition, how climatic conditions themselves changed at the beginning of the fourteenth century: a colder and much rainier climate succeeded a period of warm climate; this undoubtedly accounts for the great famine of 1315–1317, which shook all of Europe. It could be compared to the famine that, during the years 1974–1975, desolated the Sahel, not with respect to its effects (since agriculture is sufficiently differentiated in the West for local resources to be utilized, which is impossible for nomadic populations still living a pastoral life), but with respect to its causes.

Another, more subtle and probably more radical, change came from progress in the way of measuring time. It was at the beginning of the fourteenth century that the mechanical clock appeared.[7] Up until then the seasonal, biological rhythms, the succession of days and nights, that of seasons marked by liturgical feasts, formed for everyday life a texture that had nothing rigorous about it and presented very differentiated contrasts.

Thus the simple fact that one fasted twenty days before Christmas and forty days before Easter, and that the subsequent feasts thereby acquired their full spiritual and material meaning, presupposes alternations breaking any monotony. Let us add that, if all scientific progress owes something more or less to the cutting of time by the mechanical clock and its derivatives, that latter in return created a rupture of mentality that had an effect on the man of the fourteenth century in relation to the one of the thirteenth century, precisely as in our time the possibilities of measuring time more and more exactly and rigorously have had just as much effect on the rhythms of work as on athletic events.

We could go on, but these few traits are enough to stress the contrasts that exist from one period to another and which render impossible the generalizations to which we are used to consigning the gaps in our historical education.

Thus wars, famines, epidemics really do characterize these Middle Ages, those of the fourteenth and fifteenth centuries, especially in France. Our country went through at that time one of the most terrible periods of its history, although the wars were sporadic: the famous Hundred Years' War included, between 1340 and 1453, approximately sixty years of

[7] Jean Gimpel does not hesitate to see the period that runs from the fourteenth century to our own as "the era of the mechanical clock". See his work entitled *La Révolution industrielle du moyen âge*, Points (Paris: Éd. du Seuil, 1974), 141ff. Let me add that I had intended to devote a chapter to technical progress achieved in the Middle Ages, but, upon the publication of Gimpel's book, I considered it sufficient to refer the reader to it.

declared hostilities, affecting only one very restricted part of the territory; permanent disasters were caused by mercenaries, men of war employed for pay, who found a way of living on the country and whose presence was consequently dangerous for the populations, in times of peace as in times of war. To get a sound appreciation of the situation, and with some perspective, one must recall that in 1958, the French army had been "active", according to the customary euphemism, for fifty-two years, since the beginning of the century; the modern army is composed of resources from the whole nation in contrast to what happened in the Middle Ages, when the soldiers were voluntary.

All that obviously does not mean that the feudal age was exempt from the difficulties that afflict mankind in all times; but let us reflect, for example, on the fate of Paris, which experienced no attack between that of the Normans in 885–887 and the troubles of the mid-fourteenth century under Étienne Marcel: more than four hundred years transpired without the city being touched by wars or internal disorders; if we compare that with what has happened in Paris from 1789 to our own day, it is unnecessary to dwell on the total number of successive revolutions, attacks, foreign occupations . . . Without forgetting the cholera of the nineteenth century and the Spanish flu of the twentieth!

\* \* \*

Our generation finds itself at the junction of two conceptions of the world. One is that in which we have been raised and which is heir to the three or four preceding centuries: at the center of everything is erected the *homo academicus* animated by the reasoning reason and Aristotelian logic, judging according to Roman law and admitting, in the way of aesthetics, only that of classical Greco-Latin antiquity, the whole within a three-dimensional universe whose limits and components, as Berthelot could believe even as late as the last century, will soon be entirely defined. It so happened that scientific progress, determined by scientists contemporary with Berthelot, brought about a shattering of that vision; without even referring to the scientific acquisitions of today (a today that in fact goes back to the end of the last century), whether it is a matter of relativity, wave mechanics, the notion of space-time or more simply the means of exploration, pushed beyond anything that might have been foreseen only a hundred years ago, it is enough to note around us the annihilation of what one could call the classical vision of the universe.

We see this classical vision, that which could be said (very summarily) to come to us from Aristotle through Saint Thomas and Descartes, being born in the Middle Ages. It was in the thirteenth century that Aristotelian logic (Aristotle re thought by the Arab philosophers was a little at that time like Hegel is in ours for the university world) was, not without some effort, adopted by Christian philosophy; it was in the same period that a synthesis was worked out, glimpsed by Abelard but led to its conclusion a century and a half later by Thomas Aquinas and his master Albert the Great. Still, it is a pure optical error to see in this a system of thought dominating the thirteenth century: on the contrary, at the time it had the effect of a kind of foreign body that one tries to expel. It was only much later that Thomistic thought would be fully adopted; at the time it was formulated, it was far from asserting itself. Let us recall that in this same thirteenth century, Robert Grossetête founded, not only a whole aesthetic, but an order of knowledge on the study of light. And what is to be said of those thinkers of the preceding century, the twelfth, who gave life to the school of Saint-Victor in

Paris! Without feeling any need to rely on Plato or Aristotle, but not ignorant of either of them—at least in part—Hugh of Saint-Victor placed at the beginning of all contemplation that of the beauty of the universe; he assigned movement as the primary element, the source also of aesthetical pleasure: the movement of winds, waves, stars in the heavens; he presupposed a beauty invisible to our senses. Are conceptions of this kind not closer to the scientific as well as the artistic vision of our time than the one governed by the hope to reduce man and the world to definitions and classifications? An exposition that took place at the Museum of Paris in 1974 showed photographs obtained from the electronic microscope: *Nature Multiplied by 10,000*; it gave a totally unsuspected vision of the universe, curiously close, moreover, to that of so-called abstract art in its best productions: of very beautiful strips that evoked a cultivated field or a forest or wonderful geometrical constructions, turned out to be, upon consulting the label, a cutting of a hair, the tip of a bug's foot, the surface of a gnat's eye. One need hardly say that this was very far from the Cartesian universe, but certainly Hugh of Saint-Victor or Isidore of Seville would have walked with delight in the universe revealed electronically. Who was it who said, in this vein, that the classical period was the one where man placed, at the beginning of all knowledge, doubt instead of wonder? Today, the electronic microscope, like the voyage of the astronaut, could reconcile us with a time that, by instinct, accepted wonder, that did not refuse those "qualitative leaps" (the expression is that of Maurice Clavel referring to Kierkegaard) that the categories of classical logic render inadmissible.

And it is very probable that coming generations will be astonished that we could for so long a time exclude a whole period of our past, and precisely the one that left the most convincing traces of itself. Would it not be time to put an end to that systematic lack of curiosity and to admit that one can study in the field of human sciences, with neither scorn nor complex, those thousand years of our history that were something quite other than a middle term?

# 9

# SIMPLE REMARKS ON THE TEACHING OF HISTORY

Some recent—very recent—provisions seem as if they will provide a somewhat more important place than in the past for the human sciences in the education of children. The historian can only applaud this, and the educator even more. In fact, one might wonder if, up until now, the elaboration of programs was not seen much more as a function of materials to be stuffed in than as a function of the child himself and of the imperatives of his development. That observation, of course, is nothing new; all educators worthy of the name have formulated more or less the same thing. And already the efforts of all those who recommended active methods have begun to bear fruit.

But, for the historian, the imperatives are becoming more vital. The official programs, as well as the methods used in the past, actually ruled out what constitutes the proper interest of history. Let us recall, for example, the absurdity of having the history of the Middle Ages studied in high school and its literature in grammar school. This, moreover, kept a good number of teachers from teaching anything at all about the Middle Ages, historical or literary. In schools where teaching methods had developed, teachers were released from them in order to break with the program.

Another absurdity that must be stressed: the very principle that consisted in cutting history into slices—very unequal slices, at that—with the simplistic idea that what has been studied for one year is assimilated for a whole lifetime.

Does there not have to be a place for reviewing the question in its entirety by envisaging not only the study of facts but, indeed, the *formation of a historical sense* in the child, which seems as necessary as the *formation of a literary sense*.

To neglect this formation is to miss the positive contribution of the study of history.

Whether one wishes it or not, man is *also* a historical animal: the place he occupies in time is as important for him as that which he occupies in space; and this natural curiosity that each feels about his place of origin and that of his family, his parents, indeed, of his ancestors, is just as legitimate, just as justified as that of the doctor who questions his patient, not only about his childhood illnesses, but also about the conditions of his parents' life and death. It is unnecessary to insist, in the century of psychoanalysis, on the immediate interest for each of us offered by our past and that of our relatives—an interest as powerful, as deep as that of the social milieu in general, on which such emphasis is placed nowadays—an interest that extends quite naturally from the individual to the group, to the region.

But, like all initiation, all teaching, that of history should be reclothed with different forms, according to the age of the one being taught (obviously mental age: no educator is unaware that this mental age differs greatly from that of the civil status for a child, that being who is in continual but discontinuous evolution).

Why not teach history in small classes through the use of anecdotes, solely through anecdotes, destined to leave great names in the memory and unimaginable facts in the imag-

ination, as only history can furnish, well beyond any ficti-
tious legend. And do so, of course, without any concern for
chronology: everyone knows that up until the age of nine or
ten years, even later for many children, succession in time
means nothing; it is thus completely useless up until that age
to encumber the memory with dates, quite as useless as to
persist, as was done for so long a time, in making it do "anal-
yses" at a stage when the intelligence is precisely incapable
of analyzing. On the other hand, there is not a child, no
matter how young, who does not love stories, especially when
they are "true". Now at an age when what is recounted takes
root for the whole of one's life, it would be of first importance to fill minds with a historical repertory whose human
interest is inexhaustible.

A little later, around nine to twelve years, any educator
can greatly stimulate the social sense that is awakening and
also show his students how to see what surrounds us by having recourse to local history. The study of history could then
be mixed with that of the environment. This is, moreover,
what the masters formed in active methods have long called
"the study of the milieu". In order for this to be done well,
it demands a reference to history and also some explorations
that could be extremely beneficial: visits to museums, of
course, but also to archives, even if merely those of the town
mayor, as well as the study of land registers, of the civil state,
of the census . . . Finally the study of the monuments of the
past (what region of France is without them?), of people and
events that have marked the locality, eventually of excavations that might exist nearby—all that should be the subject
matter of a history course and would obviously be more educational than having to learn a textbook summary.

Finally, when the possibility of analysis and abstraction ar-
rives, one could tackle visions of history that are at once

more general and much more precise through subjects put back into their chronological and factual framework, by referring to the documents and texts of the period studied; it is obviously out of the question nowadays to limit ourselves to political and military history. History is understood only in connection with geology and geography, extending to economics, to the history of art, and so on. Textbooks can then be used with much profit, in the class library.

In addition, more generally, is it possible to conduct a serious study in any domain without having first sketched at least summarily the history of the material studied?

\* \* \*

"How can anybody be interested in history at a time when men are walking on the moon?" someone said one day.

The answer is easy. What was the first act accomplished by man once he was on the moon? He bent down to pick up a rock. The gesture of the archeologist. The first reflex of the first astronaut was also that which brings out the very material of history.

Nothing is more natural; history is life; beyond any definitions or abstractions, man is expressed by his history, and if a rock can have so much interest for him, it is because it is, literally, a "sign of life".

The Cartesian *tabula rasa* is perhaps the greatest philosophical lie of all time. It is in any case the one whose application weighs most heavily on our own time. The idea of "wiping the slate clean", of "starting from scratch" always constitutes a seductive temptation. But it is precisely an impossible enterprise: it is impossible except in a totally arbitrary view of the mind, taking no account of concrete realities. Because everything that constitutes a life is given, transmitted. One never starts from zero. Freud would serve to demonstrate this, if any such demonstration were necessary. Or again, in simpler terms, that text from Genesis which shows us each fruit "carrying its seed"—which denied in advance any spontaneous generation. It is striking to think that every time it has been transposed into facts, the temptation to "start from zero" has ended in death, in multiple deaths and destruction, and that in all domains. In the wish to make a "clean slate", how many times have we stupidly destroyed what might have been a support, a foundation stone? But it will perhaps be given to our era to rediscover the importance of tradition, which is a living given, susceptible like all life to growth, to acquisition, to enrichment from new contributions. This could be done by rediscovering the importance of history, which is the search for actual experience, that actual experience on the basis of which we lead our own life. It is the same with history as it is with archeological strata: there is always an underlying layer, and when one reaches virgin soil, the archeologist cedes the field to the geologist, who in turn retraces the history of this soil.

History is life, precisely because it includes a given, something that pre-exists our concepts, our prejudices, and our systems: the coin bearing some particular head and found at some determined place; the conclusion drawn from it can be erroneous; but the fact, the coin indicating some particular date, found in a particular place, does not depend on us; we must accept it, as we must accept that a particular manuscript was written at a particular date and on the order of some particular person—as long as the critical arsenal has been correctly put to work in establishing it.

It is true that a fashionable doctrine would like to convince me that I read in the texts what I really want to read in them. This is sometimes true: I am thinking of that writer who, in order to prove that Joan of Arc was really the "bastard of Orleans", omitted in one quotation the four lines that contradicted his assertion . . .

It is surely not necessary to stress that that is not history. History is an ascesis; I would unquestioningly say a heroic ascesis. Those who have excavated this summer, according to the expression of *Archéologia*, will freely recognize this with me—for they are closer to history than the gatherers of anecdotes and forgers of fantasies calculated to flatter opinion.

Arduous science demands bending at length over shards and unintelligible scribbles—those scribbles that the Marxist historians find easy to treat with scorn because they call into question their own existence as historians. To weigh and feel the weight of the historical value of each source of documentation, from the pottery shard to the ancient deed or notarial act, slowly to disengage the living substance from a juxtaposition of controlled facts, that which permits one to reconstitute piece by piece the itinerary of a person, his work, and at times, if one has sufficiently abundant and expressive a documentation, his mentality—that demands many years of work, and in our era of facility, it is, once again, nearly heroic, but this too merely belongs to the price of doing history. On condition, too, of having at length identified the sources, of being filled with the context so as to be able to penetrate the relative value; and that often in order to extract only a small fragment—that one might call insignificant if one were not otherwise certain, and from experience, that no small fragment of truth will ever be insignificant.

As for those who deny the importance of the documentation in itself, we will not take the trouble to refute them: if they deny it, is it not because they are themselves incapable of accepting information other than what they have formulated in advance? The question must be posed; after which one will be able profitably to invite them to come examine, for instance, a repository of archives; several miles of shelves will serve as the most good-natured contradiction to their system of thought.

The given of history is there, but it requires, of course, much time, work, and respect to explore it and to uncover, subsequently, the substance of it. It is perfectly understandable that some prefer to escape it through scorn; it is infinitely easier to develop ideas; only ignorance of the document permits the development of ideas in complete serenity, in order to draw from them historico-sociological systems satisfying for the mind.

What is fruitful in historical research is, on the contrary, that obstacle, or rather, those perpetually encountered obstacles that conflict with our prejudices and lead us to modify our biases. A starting bias is, of course, stimulating, but one must know how to resign oneself to abandoning it every time the documents dictate it.

History obliges respect, a bit like medicine or education, in short, everything concerning man; otherwise one has soon deviated from, taken away from the internal demands of the adopted discipline. One ceases to be a historian when one neglects or mutilates a document, just as one ceases to be a doctor when one scorns or underestimates the result of an analysis or examination, or just as one ceases to be an educator when one encroaches on the personality of the person one is charged with teaching.

That is perhaps the principal interest of this formation of the historical sense that is so desirable in the matter of education. At the age when the adolescent is seeking the "other", and is being formed with respect to the "other", there would be nothing more fruitful for him than this encounter with what has preceded him in time and which is, once again, as close to him, as necessary as what surrounds him in space. It is probably due to the lack of this twofold dimension, time as well as space, that so many minds remain atrophied, formed in a unilateral, summary, simplistic fashion. The study of history brings to youth the experience that is lacking to it; it can help the adolescent to overcome his most usual temptation: to be exclusive, to condemn in advance some particular tendency, person, or group; to have a vision of the universe limited only to his own vision (and if only this were a matter merely of adolescents!).

At the age when it is important to confront the values received—those of his surroundings, childhood, family, or social milieu—with his own personality, the study of history would enlarge the field of this investigation and would furnish dimensions impossible to acquire otherwise. The young today show a remarkable appetite for travel, which is a healthy reflex, but the dimension of time is lacking in their spatial universe. And this is a lacuna.

The significance of history as material for education could thus be immense for intellectual maturation. Chesterton said that a man is truly a man only when he has looked at the world while standing on his head with his feet in the air. One can practice the same kind of exercise without too much fatigue by studying history. By familiarizing oneself with other times, other eras, other civilizations, one acquires the habit of distrusting criteria of one's own time: they will evolve like others have evolved. It is the occasion for personally revising one's own thought mechanism, one's own motives for action or reflection by comparison with those of others. There is in that an enlargement of the familiar horizon that can be extremely beneficial, on condition, of course, that it is a matter of true history and not simply of the prefabricated judgments distributed so generously in teaching.

The study of history allows us, finally, to situate the notion of progress accurately. We generally have a very elementary idea of progress. As Lewis Mumford writes, one is led to think that, if the streets of our cities were dirty in the nineteenth century, they must have been six hundred times dirtier six hundred years earlier. How many students believe with good faith that what happened in the nineteenth century (for example, the work of children in factories) had always existed and that only the class struggle and the trade unions at the end of the nineteenth century freed humanity from this fault! How many militants in the feminist movements think in good faith that women have always been confined in an at least moral gynaeceum, and that only the progress of our twentieth century has accorded them some freedom of expression, of work, and of personal life! For the historian, the general progress is not in doubt: but no less the fact that it is never a question of continuous, uniform, determined progress. That humanity advances on some points, regresses on others, and all the more easily as a particular impulse that effects progress at some given moment will subsequently cause a regression. In the sixteenth century it was in no way doubted that humanity was making progress, and particularly from the economic point of view; very few people were aware of what, as Las Cases and some other Dominican friars of the New World were proclaiming, this economic progress was doing in reestablishing slavery through a gigantic reactionary movement and that, in consequence, one step forward here was being paid for by a recession elsewhere. Humanity indisputably progresses, but neither uniformly nor everywhere.

Finally, outside even questions of education, where its role should be capital, where it should even serve as the structure for all teaching, there is a general profit in history. We are far

from any idea of an eternal beginning or even of very artificial, subjective, and arbitrary comparisons between one period and another; farther still from thinking that history might
bring a solution to the problems of the day: if one can draw
any conclusion from the study of history it is, on the contrary, that the solution of yesterday is *never* that of today. The
armed pilgrimage that we call the crusades was well and truly,
whether one likes it or not, the indispensable solution at the
end of the eleventh century for coming to the aid of the
Holy Places and the Near East in general—but already this
was no longer the solution called for at the beginning of the
thirteenth century and even less at the end of that same thirteenth century, and it is striking to note that no attention
was given by the powers of that time to someone like Ramon Lull, who was indicating the solution of the day when,
in the West, the popes, emperors, and kings unflaggingly
went back to the solution of the prior age.[1] But are we not
much more at ease formulating such judgments when we
benefit from hindsight? . . .

History does not furnish any solution, but it permits—
and it alone permits—us to pose the problems correctly. Now
everyone knows that a problem correctly posed is already
half solved. History alone permits this because it alone au-
thorizes the inventory of a given situation; it alone furnishes
the elements from which this situation results. There is no
true knowledge without recourse to history. And it is true

---

[1] Ramon Lull, that genius, poet, and prophet, had advocated another type
of expedition into the land of Islam: doctors, nurses, and also preachers capable of expressing themselves in the language of the "Saracens". He was at the
origin of the creation of colleges of Oriental languages, the first of which was
proposed at the time of the Council of Vienne in 1312. Refer to the work by
Ramon Sugranyes de Franch, *Raymond Lulle docteur des missions* (Fribourg,
1954).

everywhere that man, the life of man, is at issue. One knows a living body only by its history. In neglecting the formation of a historical sense, by forgetting that history is the memory of peoples, instruction forms amnesiacs. Schools and universities are sometimes reproached nowadays for forming irresponsible people, by favoring the intellect to the detriment of sensibility and character. But it is serious also to create amnesiacs. The amnesiac is no more a complete person than an irresponsible person is; neither one enjoys the full exercise of his faculties, which alone allow man true freedom without endangering himself or his peers.

# INDEX